THE EVERYTHING
LARGE-PRINT TV
WORD SEARCH BOOK

Dear Reader,

TV is looking better than ever. I've never had so much fun watching "the tube" (as we used to call it). Thanks to today's technology, there is an abundance of really good programs. I'm also a puzzle person, so it was a pleasure to combine two things I love: television and word searches.

Like a favorite TV show, a word search puzzle is a nice way to relax and escape from the real world. But you don't have to wait for next week's episode when you want more puzzles. There are enough here to keep your brain happy for a long time.

We printed this book using large letters to make solving the puzzles more pleasant. It's kind of like watching television on a giant screen—everything is bigger. Each puzzle has a theme that is somehow related to television, from the past to the present. I hope your journey through these pages is rewarding and fun!

Charles Timmerman

Welcome to the EVERYTHING® Series!

These handy, accessible books give you all you need to tackle a difficult project, gain a new hobby, comprehend a fascinating topic, prepare for an exam, or even brush up on something you learned back in school but have since forgotten.

You can choose to read an Everything® book from cover to cover or just pick out the information you want from our four useful boxes: e-questions, e-facts, e-alerts, and e-ssentials. We give you everything you need to know on the subject, but throw in a lot of fun stuff along the way, too.

We now have more than 400 Everything® books in print, spanning such wide-ranging categories as weddings, pregnancy, cooking, music instruction, foreign language, crafts, pets, New Age, and so much more. When you're done reading them all, you can finally say you know Everything®!

PUBLISHER Karen Cooper

MANAGING EDITOR, EVERYTHING® SERIES Lisa Laing

COPY CHIEF Casey Ebert

ASSISTANT PRODUCTION EDITOR Alex Guarco

ACQUISITIONS EDITOR Lisa Laing

EVERYTHING® SERIES COVER DESIGNER Erin Alexander

Visit the entire Everything® series at *www.everything.com*

THE EVERYTHING LARGE-PRINT TV WORD SEARCH BOOK

Large-print word search puzzles for super TV fans

Charles Timmerman
Founder of Funster.com

Adams Media
New York   London   Toronto   Sydney   New Delhi

Adams Media
An Imprint of Simon & Schuster, Inc.
100 Technology Center Drive
Stoughton, MA 02072

An Everything® Series Book.
Everything® and everything.com® are registered trademarks of Simon & Schuster, Inc.

ADAMS MEDIA and colophon are trademarks of Simon and Schuster.

For information about special discounts for bulk purchases, please contact Simon & Schuster Special Sales at 1-866-506-1949 or business@simonandschuster.com.

The Simon & Schuster Speakers Bureau can bring authors to your live event. For more information or to book an event contact the Simon & Schuster Speakers Bureau at 1-866-248-3049 or visit our website at www.simonspeakers.com.

Manufactured in the United States of America

13 2022

ISBN 978-1-4405-6683-7

Acknowledgments

I would like to thank each and every one of the more than half a million people who have visited my website, *www.funster.com*, to play word games and puzzles. You have shown me how much fun puzzles can be and how addictive they can become!

It is a pleasure to acknowledge the folks at Adams Media who made this book possible. I particularly want to thank my editor, Lisa Laing, for so skillfully managing the many projects we have worked on together.

Contents

Introduction

The puzzles in this book are in the traditional word search format. Words in the list are hidden in the puzzle in any direction: up, down, forward, backward, or diagonal. The words are always found in a straight line, and letters are never skipped. Words can overlap. For example, the two letters at the end of the word "MAST" could be used as the start of the word "STERN." Only uppercased letters are used, and any spaces in an entry are removed. For example, "TROPICAL FISH" would be found in the puzzle as "TROPICALFISH." Apostrophes and hyphens are also omitted in the puzzles. Draw a circle around each word that you find. Then cross the word off the list so that you will always know which words remain to be found.

A favorite strategy is to look for the first letter in a word, then see if the second letter is in any of the neighboring letters, and so on until the word is found. Or instead of searching for the first letter in a word, it is sometimes easier to look for letters that stand out, like Q, *U*, *X*, and *Z*. Double letters in a word will also stand out and be easier to find. Another strategy is to simply scan each row, column, and diagonal looking for any words.

Puzzles

BORED	RELAXING
BROWSE	REMOTE
CABLE	RERUN
CHANGE	ROMANTIC
COMEDY	SCAN
DECISION	SEEK
DRAMA	SHIFT
EPISODES	SHOWS
FIGHTS	SITCOM
GAME	SKIM
GLANCE	SPORTS
GLIMPSE	STATION
GUIDE	SURVEY
HOPPING	SWITCH
KIDS	TELETHON
MUSIC	VIEW
NETWORKS	WATCH
NEWS	WEATHER
PERUSE	
PROGRAM	
RANDOM	
RECORD	

```
W C Y E V R U S T R O P S M
A G U I D E F D R O C E R U
T L R E L A X I N G E R S S
C A Z N E T W O R K S U K I
H N N I E P I S O D E S I C
C C O V E S H M M O V E M A
T E H I I S A G A D E R O B
I W T C T E P S N R S C D L
W S E K S A W M T I G C N E
S D L A R W T J I H P O A K
H I E Z T X E S C L G P R N
I K T J C H A N G E G I O P
F G O C Y D E M O C L E F H
T A M K O F B R O W S E G I
H M E M A M A R D S H O W S
R E R U N G V B G Z Q Q M Z
```

Solution on Page 300

ALICE

ANGIE

BARETTA

BENSON

CANNON

CARD SHARKS

CLUE CLUB

DANCE FEVER

DELTA HOUSE

FAMILY FEUD

FISH

FLASH GORDON

FLIP

GOOD TIMES

HAPPY DAYS

HART TO HART

HOUSE CALLS

JEANNIE

KUNG FU

LOTSA LUCK

MAUDE

POLICE STORY

POLICE WOMAN

RHODA

SCTV

SHA NA NA

SOAP

SPEED BUGGY

STAR TREK

TATTLETALES

TAXI

THE OSMONDS

```
C K E R T R A T S U F F Y S
L C A N N O N E F D L I G E
U U E D U A M G U A I S G L
E L T A X I N E S N P H U A
C A H S T U F H P C D U B T
L S E D K Y G S O E H P D E
U T O T L O H B L F C O E L
B O S I R A K T I E A L E T
G L M D N A A S C V R I P T
L A O A A H H I E E D C S A
F N N A O D L O S R S E E T
S A D U D A O O T V H W I T
N O S N E B Y H O T A O G E
J E A N N I E C R C R M N R
G H A P P Y D A Y S K A A A
K H O U S E C A L L S N H B
```

Solution on Page 300

ACHIEVEMENT

ALLISON

ANDREW COSBY

BREAKTHROUGHS

CARTER

CHRIS GAUTHIER

CLASSIFIED

COLIN FERGUSON

ECCENTRIC

ERICA CERRA

EXPERIMENT

GENIUS

HENRY

INTELLECTUAL

JACK

JAIME PAGLIA

JOE MORTON

JORDAN HINSON

NEIL GRAYSTON

NIALL MATTER

PENTAGON

POWER

REMOTE

SECRET

SMART HOUSE

TOWN

ZANE

ZOE

```
N O S U G R E F N I L O C K
I R J O E M O R T O N H E C
A E A Y B S O C W E R D N A
L T I T T X X S L I B H N J
L R M E O X U H S E T E O L
M A E R W I S G S C I R T A
A C P C N E A U N L D I N U
T H A E Z U O O G A C C E T
T I G S T H S R N S I A M C
E E L H T I A H O S R C I E
R V I R L Y I T G I T E R L
S E A L S N Y K A F N R E L
R M A T S L R A T I E R P E
S E O O Z A N E N E C A X T
C N N P O W E R E D C S E N
E T O M E R H B P Y E M Z I
```

Solution on Page 300

ALAN ALDA

BARNEY MILLER

BOB NEWHART

CAROL BURNETT

CHEERS

DINAH SHORE

DRAGNET

FRASIER

GET SMART

I LOVE LUCY

LOST

LOU GRANT

MAD MEN

MODERN FAMILY

MURPHY BROWN

PICKET FENCES

SEINFELD

TAXI

THE COSBY SHOW

THE DAILY SHOW

THE DEFENDERS

THE OFFICE

THE PRACTICE

THE SOPRANOS

THE WEST WING

```
T H E S O P R A N O S Y F D
R A R Y C U L E V O L I L U
A M O T H E O F F I C E I B
H U H F E T S E M T F T A S
W R S R E T T A A N H R S E
E P H A R E F X I E N D R C
N H A S S N I E C E U Z E N
B Y N I R R S O Y W Y Z D E
O B I E Y U S M A D M E N F
B R D R R B I D R A G N E T
W O H S Y L I A D E H T F E
M W H S L O U G R A N T E K
I N H E T R A M S T E G D C
C O R A L A N A L D A D E I
W E C I T C A R P E H T H P
E Z G N I W T S E W E H T T
```

Solution on Page 300

ANALYSIS

ANCHOR

ANNOUNCE

BREAKING

BRIEF

BULLETIN

CHANNELS

CHARITY

CIVIC

COVERAGE

CRIME

DESK

DETAILS

EARLY

EVENTS

FIELD

LATE

LIVE

LOCAL

MESSAGE

MONEY

MORNING

NATIONAL

NEWSROOM

NOON

OPINION

PIECE

POLICE

REPORT

SCHOOL

SCOOP

SPORTS

STORY

TALK

TELECAST

TRAFFIC

UPDATE

WARNING

WEATHER

WORLD

```
S W O R L D U V H G K G U E
T R O P E R O H C N A F V T
O K Y T I R A H C I V I C A
R B E O P I N I O N L E S L
Y C R I M E K X V R E L I K
Y F L I N S M Q E A T D S N
Y S T N E V E B R W A X Y S
L C S D W F S U A N D S L C
R H A D S Y S L G O P G A O
A O C E R E A L E O U N N O
E O E T O N G E R N N I A P
C L L A O O E T A O N K G O
E O E I M M S I U E T A L L
I C T L G N I N R O M E H I
P A T S H G C I F F A R T C
N L D G R E H T A E W B R E
```

Solution on Page 301

ANOTHER WORLD

BEN CASEY

BIRDMAN

DARK SHADOWS

F TROOP

FLIPPER

GET SMART

GIDGET

GREEN ACRES

I SPY

JONNY QUEST

MISTER ED

PEYTON PLACE

ROGER RAMJET

SECRET AGENT

SPACE GHOST

STAR TREK

THE AVENGERS

THE BEATLES

THE DOCTORS

THE FUGITIVE

THE INVADERS

THE MUNSTERS

THE PRISONER

TOP CAT

22

```
J S T H E D O C T O R S G Y
K E S Z L G E T S M A R T P
D L O K T F L I P P E R V S
F T H E A V E N G E R S D I
T A G R F G F P N Y F L E S
H E E T O P C A T T R B S R
E B C R Y G C Q R O E I R E
P E A A L R E O W N I R E D
R H P T E F O R C P S D T A
I T S S P P E A R L Y M S V
S W O D A H S K R A D A N N
O M I S T E R E D C M N U I
N E P O Y G I D G E T J M E
E T N E G A T E R C E S E H
R A J E V I T I G U F E H T
P M U J O N N Y Q U E S T P
```

Solution on Page 301

BODY

BOSS

BRILLIANT

BY THE BOOK

CALIFORNIA

CASE

CBI

CONSULTANT

COWORKER

CRIME

DAUGHTER

DEAD

DEDUCTIONS

DETECTIVE

FAMILY

HOMICIDE

INVESTIGATOR

KILLER

KIMBALL

LISBON

METHODS

MURDER

OBSERVATION

OFFICER

OUTSMART

OWAIN YEOMAN

PARTNERSHIP

PLOYS

POLICE

PSYCHIC

RED

SIMON BAKER

TEAM

TIM KANG

TRAPS

WAYNE

WIFE

```
W I F E R E K A B N O M I S
S E N B R I L L I A N T B D
N Y K V E D I C I M O H O O
K O O B E H T Y B O G T S H
I D I L R S C A S E N R S T
M A E T P E T P V Y A A P E
B U C D A U K I S N K M A M
A G R D U V T R G I M S R G
L H I D E C R Y O A I T T G
L T M B E A T E D W T U N U
I E E T C R D I S O O O O E Y
S R E C I F F O O B B C R L
B D T N A T L U S N O C S I
O E E G Y C I H C Y S P H M
N E T R C A L I F O R N I A
K I L L E R W E C I L O P F
```

Solution on Page 301

ANTENNA

BAND

COMPRESSION

DBS

DIGITAL

DIRECT

DOWNLINK

ECHOSTAR

EKRAN

ELLIPTICAL

ENCRYPTION

EQUATOR

FEEDHORN

FOCAL POINT

FREQUENCY

HOME

LNB

MICROWAVES

MULTIPLEX

NETWORK

NTSC

ORBIT

OUTDOOR

PARABOLIC

RECEPTION

REFLECTOR

SCRAMBLED

SERVICE

SIGNAL

SYNCOM

TRANSMITTED

TRANSPONDERS

TUNED

WAVEGUIDE

```
S L C K N I L N W O D N A B
Y S N S F R E Q U E N C Y B
N R C K T V R A T S O H C E
C O Q R R N H T S I G N A L
O T I L A O I O U T D O O R
M A P S N M W O M J S I F R
L U A A S O B T P E E T E O
A Q R N P E I L E L V P E T
C E A T O K R T E N A E D C
I R B E N R S P P D W C H E
T T O N D A B E M Y O E O L
P C L N E N D I R O R R R F
I E I A R B N L T V C C N E
L R C U S L A T I G I D N R
L I X E L P I T L U M C T E
E D I U G E V A W T U N E D
```

Solution on Page 301

AWARDS

BASEBALL

CABLE

CASUAL

CHANNELS

CHIPS

COMEDY

COUCH

DATE

DRAMA

DRINKS

DVR

EVENT

FINALE

FUN

GAME

GOLF

GUESTS

HOME

HOST

LAUGH

MOVIE

NEWS

NIGHT

PARADE

POPCORN

REALITY

RECORD

REMOTE

SEATS

SERIES

SHARE

SHOW

SNACKS

SODA

SPORTS

TEARS

UNWIND

VISIT

WATCH

```
P C A S U A L X E M P A B Y
Q N I B P I W P D R A M A T
D L L M H C H A N N E L S E
X V Y T I L A E R D A T E A
L I X D V R A K O D B Y B R
A S T S E U G D C X S A A S
L I H U L M F R P H K T L E
F T C S A U O O O G N C L R
S L C H N N R C P U I W T I
W Q O W I A M E P A R A D E
S O I G F P C R M L D T W S
O N H S H W S K C O U C H T
D T M S T R O P S G T H N E
A S W E N A T C A B L E M L
K O S H A R E M E I V O M N
Z H N M N C E S H E H R N L
```

Solution on Page 302

BAKER

BIRD

CHARLOTTE

DEATH

DESTINY

DETECTIVE

DOG

ECCENTRIC

EMERSON

FATE

FIELD

FRIEND

GOOD DEED

JEALOUSY

JIM DALE

JUSTICE

LEE PACE

LILY

LOVE

MEMORY

MORGUE

MURDER

NED

OLIVE

PIE

SUPERNATURAL

SURREALISM

SWIMMING

SWOOSIE KURTZ

SY RICHARDSON

VIVIAN

WAITRESS

YOUNG

```
M E M O R Y S U O L A E J T
T C U D L I A G Q X M T R W
X J I M D A L E O E A T D H
L S Y R I C H A R D S O N T
I W W E T A F S E V O L E A
L I K O G N O F B H M R I E
Y M E B O N E B I E S A R D
O M C A O S R C V E I H F E
U I I K D E I I C K L C M S
N N T E D K T E M E A D S T
G G S R E C K X K O E E P I
T S U P E R N A T U R A L N
A M J T D R I B L T R G P Y
Z L E E P A C E I P U T U D
A D K V I V I A N Q S W Z E
D Q Q I G M W O L I V E K N
```

Solution on Page 302

ACCENT

ATLANTA

BELLE

BLANCHE

BROOKLYN

CATHOLIC

CULT TV

DATING

DAUGHTER

DIVORCEE

DOROTHY

ELDERLY

FLORIDA

FRIEND

GEORGIA

HOME

HOUSE

INSULT

ISSUES

ITALIAN

KITCHEN

MIAMI

MOTHER

NEW YORK

OLDER

PASTEL

PRIEST

ROOMMATE

ROSE

SARCASM

SENIOR

SICILY

SINGLE

SITCOM

SOCIAL

SOPHIA

TEACHER

TEMPER

WIDOW

```
M T B V O I R E H C A E T D
B S S P L T I L S C J B O I
K E A Y D A S D S L H R W S
S I L C E L S E O E O O O I
E R T L R I U R P T U O D C
N P L C E A E L H S S K I I
I E U X H N S Y I A E L W L
O M S T N E C C A P O Y E Y
R O N C R W N K E H E N T A
M H I U E Y R E T H G U A D
O G E L H O C A C T L T M I
C N L T T R C N E A N T M R
T I G T O K A M I A M I O O
I T N V M L P C L N I S O L
S A I B B E O T D N E I R F
H D S D R S A I G R O E G F
```

Solution on Page 302

ANKLE MONITOR

CAPTURED

CASE

CHARMING

CLINTON

CRIME

DIANA

ELIZABETH

ESCAPE

EVIDENCE

FBI

FORGER

GENIUS

HILARIE BURTON

INFORMATION

INVESTIGATION

MANHATTAN

MASTERMIND

MATT BOMER

NEAL

NEW YORK CITY

PARTNERSHIP

PETER

RICH

SARA

SHARIF ATKINS

SURVEILLANCE

THIEF

TIM DEKAY

TRUST

WILLIE GARSON

```
E T S G N I M R A H C S D W
C E S Y O A E G M R N I N I
N V O U T G T A E I A F E L
A I R D R I T T K N E S A L
L D N O U T C T A I I N L I
L E F V B C A K H H K U N E
I N M O E F L T R L N F S G
E C M I I S E I E O O A E A
V E G R R B T M N R Y P M R
R G A E A C O I M T A W G S
U H T Z L N B A G C O C E O
S E I R I F T E S A C N L N
P L I T H I D E R U T P A C
E C O Y O Y A K E D M I T H
H R D N I M R E T S A M O C
O C P I H S R E N T R A P N
```

Solution on Page 302

ABC

ALI FEDOTOWSKY

ASHLEE FRAZIER

ASHLEY HEBERT

CEREMONY

CHRIS HARRISON

DATES

DEANNA PAPPAS

ELIGIBLE

EXOTIC

FAMILY

HOST

JAKE PAVELKA

JENNI CROFT

JILLIAN HARRIS

KACIE BOGUSKIE

LINDSAY YENTER

LINDZI COX

MARRIAGE

NICKI STERLING

PROPOSE

REALITY

ROSE

SEAN LOWE

VISITS

WEDDING

WIFE

WOMEN

```
J S C B G R E A L I T Y E E
A R H G N I D D E W F G G I
K L R L I N D Z I C O X A K
E J I L L I A N H A R R I S
P H S F R W O M E N C V R U
A S H L E E F R A Z I E R G
V E A O T D W Y R S N C A O
E L R F S A O O I U N I M B
L B R A I T S T L Z E T Y E
K I I M K E S S O N J O P I
A G S I C S E F I W A X A C
B I O L I P R O P O S E V A
C L N Y N O M E R E C K S K
D E A N N A P A P P A S Y I
R E T N E Y Y A S D N I L O
B T R E B E H Y E L H S A N
```

Solution on Page 303

ADAM CAROLLA

ARSENIO HALL

CONAN

CRAIG FERGUSON

DAILY SHOW

DAVID FROST

DENNIS MILLER

DICK CAVETT

EMOTIONAL

GENRE

GERALDO

GUESTS

HOST

ISSUE

JIMMY FALLON

JIMMY KIMMEL

JOHNNY CARSON

JON STEWART

LENO

MIKE DOUGLAS

OPRAH

POLITICS

SPORTSCENTER

THE VIEW

TOM SNYDER

TONIGHT SHOW

TOPICS

```
K D T T R A W E T S N O J D
W D O A D A M C A R O L L A
J I M M Y K I M M E L O C I
R C S S S J B R R L D R J L
D K N C C D S N A L A I J Y
A C Y I I W E N A I M S L S
V A D T P G O R G M B S L H
I V E I O I E F Y S I U A O
D E R L T G E F X I B E H W
F T N O S R A C Y N N H O J
R T M P G L A C O N A N I G
O E V U L W E I V E H T N U
S L S O P R A H Y D I O E E
T O N I G H T S H O W N S S
N S P O R T S C E N T E R T
Q K U M I K E D O U G L A S
```

Solution on Page 303

BLOOD

BOBBY

BROTHERHOOD

CASTIEL

CROWLEY

DADDY

DEAN

DEMON

DESTINY

ERIC KRIPKE

EVIL

FATHER

FIGHTING

FRIEND

GHOST

GODS

GUN

HUNTERS

JIM BEAVER

JOHN

KILLER

LUCIFER

MACABRE

MADNESS

MEMORY

MONSTER

MURDER

OSRIC CHAU

RESCUE

RUBY

SAM

SCREAM

SEARCH

SHOOTING

SPIRIT

STABBING

SUSPENSE

VIOLENCE

WINCHESTER

WRATH

```
S D T S O H G T M E M O R Y
A E A B O B B Y N I T S E D
M A C A B R E F I C U L D N
A N S P I R I T I B W S R E
D S T A B B I N G O L D U I
N H U A H C C I R S O O M R
E O N M A E R C S O E G O F
S O H R E T S E H C N I W D
S T O E K P I R K C I R E A
E I J I M B E A V E R C S D
A N F A T H E R G U N E N D
R G N I T H G I F E R U E Y
C R J O F R E L L I K C P B
H H R E T S N O M E D S S U
S B C A S T I E L I V E U R
W R A T H V H U N T E R S M
```

Solution on Page 303

ABC

ANCHOR

ASSOCIATE

CASEY

CHRIS

CSC

DAN

ELLIOTT

EXECUTIVE

FICTIONAL

FRIENDSHIP

GREG BAKER

ISAAC

JEFF MOORING

JEREMY

JOSH CHARLES

JOSHUA MALINA

KAYLA BLAKE

KIM

LUTHER SACHS

NATALIE

NEWS

OFFICE

PETER KRAUSE

PRESSURE

PRODUCE

PROGRAM

RATINGS

RON OSTROW

SITCOM

STUDIO

TELEVISION

WILL

WORKPLACE

```
C O I D U T S I T C O M S P
A P R O N O S T R O W J I R
S Y E E C A L P K R O W R E
E M K L U T H E R S A C H S
Y E A N C H O R H B Y S C S
P R B P R O D U C E E Y F U
E E G D A N A T A L I E R R
T J E F F M O O R I N G I E
E S R K A Y L A B L A K E L
R W G L I L H C A A S I N L
K E I F I C T I O N A L D I
R N M W H S R A T I N G S O
A A S S O C I A T E B K H T
U N O I S I V E L E T N I T
S J C Y Q W M A R G O R P M
E X E C U T I V E C I F F O
```

Solution on Page 303

ACCENT	MURDER
ADDICTION	PAM
ALCIDE	PERVERSION
ANDY	PREJUDICE
ARLENE	PSYCHIC
BAR	RELATIONSHIP
BILL	RYAN KWANTEN
BLOOD	SAM
BOOK	SOOKIE
ERIC	SOUTHERN
EXORCISM	STEVE
GORE	TARA
GOTHIC	TERRY
HOLLY	TODD LOWE
HOYT	VAMPIRE
JASON	VIOLENCE
JESSICA	WAITRESS
LAFAYETTE	WEREWOLF
LAUREN BOWLES	
LOUISIANA	
LOVE	
MELODRAMA	

```
E D I C L A W E R E W O L F
G O T H I C Y P L O R A B E
X A D D I C T I O N U S C H
K O O B N E L H V R M N O T
M K E F E N L S E N E L R A
A E C T T T I N R L L A C R
S X I O N E B O O Y O N E A
O O D D A O T I G W D D K N
U R U D W W V T E R R Y V A
T C J L K A B A E U A A H I
H I E O N I S L M Y M J O S
E S R W A T T E O P A M Y I
R M P E Y R E R I O E F T U
N O I S R E V R E P D R A O
Y A C I S S E J A S O N I L
C I H C Y S P S O O K I E C
```

Solution on Page 304

ACTRESS

BAR

BIKER

BUSINESSES

CALIFORNIA

CHARMING

CHIBS

CLAY

CLUB

DOCTOR

FILTHY PHIL

GANG

GARAGE

GEMMA

HAPPY

IRISH

JAX

JOURNAL

JUICE

KATEY SAGAL

KIM COATES

LYLA

MAGGIE SIFF

MOTORCYCLE

OPIE

PIERMONT

POLICE

PRISON

ROBERT

RON PERLMAN

RYAN HURST

SAMCRO

SHERIFF

TARA

THEO ROSSI

TIG

TOWN

VETERAN

VIOLENT

WAYNE

```
H X A J W A Y N E J U I C E
A C L U B A R P R I S O N C
P T R E B O R Q H S I R I I
P N Y M A G G I E S I F F L
Y O A T H E O R O S S I C O
J M N M J Z T I G E L H V P
O R H B L C K V S T I C I Q
U E U I A R E S H B L H O K
R I R K A T E Y S A G A L I
I N P S E E N P P Y P R R E M
A O T R I H C G N A G M N C
L Z A S I D O C T O R I T O
Y N U L C A L I F O R N I A
L B U A M M E G A R A G T T
T O W N M O T O R C Y C L E
S A M C R O Q F F I R E H S
```

Solution on Page 304

AMC	HLN
BET	HSN
BIO	HTV
BOSTEL	IFC
BRAVO	MGM HD
CENTRIC	MSNBC
CHILLER	OXYGEN
CINEMAX	QUBO
CLOO	QVC
CNN	REELZ
CREATE	SPEED
DOC	SPIKE
ENCORE	STARZ
EPIX	STYLE
ESPN	SYFY
FEARNET	TBS
FLIX	TLC
FUSE	TNT
GAC	
GSN	
HBO	
HISTORY	

```
M Z A C X W Y X E C Z L C N
K P T Y Y F Y S I A T V P T
G D M K Q G T D W P A S C L
C S L G G A E H A C E F O D
A L C C R C N M R X L X H N
N Y J Z C S R G A I Y O B H
V O R C G Y A M X G T I O N
S R P O E P E M E H S B O V
E G S W T N F N C T L S R T
W G P G I S T A L V A E E B
C Q I C P H I R C H E E L E
D F K E B J C H I L L E R T
C A E Q T N T O Z C T O B C
X D C U F U S E D S C S R V
U A Y B L I M M O N N C I Q
C P D O V A R B E M H H F N
```

Solution on Page 304

ARLO

ART MULLEN

AVA

BENNETT

BOYD

COURTHOUSE

COUSIN

CRIMINAL

CROWDER

DEPUTY

DRAMA

ELMORE LEONARD

ERICA TAZEL

FAMILY FEUD

FEDERAL

FX NETWORK

GRAHAM YOST

HOMETOWN

JACOB PITTS

JOELLE CARTER

JOHNNY

KENTUCKY

LAWMAN

MARSHAL

NATALIE ZEA

NICK SEARCY

RACHEL

SHOOT

TIM

TOUGH

WALTON GOGGINS

WESTERN

WINONA

```
A T T E N N E B O L R A F W
O N S S T T I P B O C A J E
E H O M E T O W N R M R Y S
S L Y N N H O J O I E T A T
U A M T I M L W L T U M O E
O H A O R W D Y R P A U C R
H S H O R E F A E R G L R N
T R A H R E C D D H N L I I
R A R S U E L B O Y D E M C
U M G D L A R E D E F N I K
O W A L T O N G O G G I N S
C V E K R O W T E N X F A E
A O A E Z E I L A T A N L A
J Y Z L E Z A T A C I R E R
N I S U O C N A M W A L D C
R A C H E L K E N T U C K Y
```

Solution on Page 304

ADMIRER

ADORE

ATHLETE

AUTOGRAPH

BANNER

CELEBRITY

CHEER

CLUB

COLLEGE

COLORS

COMMITTED

CONCERT

COWBOYS

DEDICATED

DEVOUT

FANATIC

FANDOM

FANZINE

FOLLOWER

GROUPIE

IDOLIZE

JERSEY

LOUD

LOYAL

MANIAC

MASCOT

MUSICIAN

NASCAR

OBSESSED

ONLOOKER

PARTY

PENNANT

SIGN

SPORTS

STAR

SUPPORT

TEAM

TICKET

TREKKIES

```
M A S C O T J M O D N A F S
C C D F O L L O W E R Y A P
B I E O S M U S I C I A N O
O K T L R R M L A Y O L Z R
B F A A E E O I T E K C I T
A G C E N B N L T E A M N S
N K I H P A R G O T U A E T
N S D T M U F I I C E A V A
E C E J R D S Q T S G D P R
R Z D I E E G U D Y E M E P
P C I V K R C K P S L I N R
A L O L O K S N S P L R N A
R U D U O L E E O H O E A C
T B P C L D S R Y C C R N S
Y I G R N B I E T E L H T A
E S S Y O B W O C H E E R N
```

Solution on Page 305

APPLIANCE

AUDIENCE

BREAK

CAMPAIGN

CARS

CHANNEL

CLEANERS

CLOTHING

DEAL

DIAPER

DISPLAY

DOCTOR

FOOD

FUNNY

GAMES

GOODS

HOTELS

IMPULSE

JINGLE

LAWYER

MEALS

MEDIA

MUSIC

NETWORK

PEDDLE

PITCH

PREVIEW

PRICE

PRODUCT

RATINGS

SALES

SELLING

SERVICE

SHIPPING

SLOGAN

SNACKS

STATION

STORES

TOYS

TRAVEL

```
G E L D D E P M E D I A L D
O H K A E R B P R I C E E M
O O R Q W D S A L E S A U F
D T A D F Y I M P U L S E X
S E C I V R E S G N I T A R
L L W E I V E R P C A R S E
O S F P G S C A P L C H E P
G Y O I N H L P R F A Q R A
A O O T I I E P O U M Y O I
N T D C H P A L D N P D T D
O J T H T P N I U N A O S S
I I R A O I E A C Y I C N L
T N A N L N R N T Q G T A A
A G V N C G S C G O N O C E
T L E E T H N E T W O R K M
S E L L I N G A M E S R S B
```

Solution on Page 305

AL FRANKEN

AMY POEHLER

BAND

BELUSHI

BILL MURRAY

CAREERS

CELEBRITY

CHEVY CHASE

CHRIS ROCK

COMIC

CULT TV

DAN AYKROYD

DANA CARVEY

DAVID SPADE

DON PARDO

HOST

IRREVERENCE

JACK HANDEY

JON LOVITZ

LATE NIGHT

LIVE

MIKE MYERS

NEWS

NORA DUNN

PARODY

POLITICS

SATIRE

SKETCH

SKITS

SLAPSTICK

SNL

SONG

TINA FEY

```
T C E C L A T E N I G H T C
I A P C D S L A P S T I C K
N R A D N A B F S K E T C H
A E R S W E N E R I T A S O
F E O Y E V R A C A N A D D
E R D S S S T E Y I N C T R
Y S Y A J R A T V K M K K A
E A M Y P O E H L E R O E P
D V R S Y S N Y C U R O C N
N P I R N P D L M Y C R Y O
A B E L U S H I O E V R I D
H O S T K M C V V V K E E U
K S C I T I L O P A I I H R
C Y T I R B E L E C D T M C
A S F K C O R S I R H C Z V
J N N U D A R O N B G N O S
```

Solution on Page 305

BEN GAZZARA

BILL COSBY

BRUCE WILLIS

CARL BETZ

DAMIAN LEWIS

DAVID CARUSO

DENNIS FRANZ

EDWARD ASNER

HAL HOLBROOK

JACK KLUGMAN

JAMES GARNER

JAMES SPADER

JERRY ORBACH

JIM DAVIS

JON HAMM

KIRK DOUGLAS

LARRY HAGMAN

MARTIN SHEEN

MIKE CONNORS

RALPH WAITE

ROB LOWE

RON LEIBMAN

```
J E R R Y O R B A C H L J T
A M I K E C O N N O R S F P
M A R T I N S H E E N V L X
E S R Z B E N G A Z Z A R A
S A D N A M G U L K K C A J
S L H A L H O L B R O O K A
P G E R M S I V A D M I J M
A U W F B I L L C O S B Y E
D O O S U R A C D I V A D S
E D L I V J O N H A M M W G
R K B N Z T E B L R A C J A
N R O N N A M B I E L N O R
I I R E N S A D R A W D E N
M K G D R A L P H W A I T E
P W B R U C E W I L L I S R
Y L A R R Y H A G M A N D Q
```

Solution on Page 305

BAT

BRETT

BRUCE HELFORD

CHARLIE

COMEDY

COUNSELOR

DAUGHTER

FATHER

FILM

FRIEND

GAME

GROUP

INJURY

INSTRUCTOR

JENNIFER

KATE

LACEY

MARTIN

MICHAEL

NEIGHBOR

NOLAN

NOUREEN DEWULF

PAROLE

PATIENT

PATRICK

PRISON

SAM

SELMA BLAIR

SHAWNEE SMITH

SITCOM

SUCCESSFUL

TEENAGE

THERAPY

60

```
X M A R T I N J U R Y D F W
M O C T I S K A T E U L Q L
O D R O F L E H E C U R B E
M L I F D X U F I W Q R T A
M A S H A W N E E S M I T H
K C I R T A P D K B P A H C
I E N R R P N O L A N L E I
D Y S N O E R E T T U B R M
D P T M E L F I G F H A A L
Y A R R D I E I S A N M P P
L R U F G N G S N O N L Y R
M O C G T A E H N N N E D E
N L T R H C M I B U E S E H
H E O O C T D E R O O J M T
U L R U T T E R B F R C O A
G A S P E I L R A H C H C F
```

WCCB	WKCF
WCET	WKEF
WCIA	WKHA
WCLF	WKLE
WCML	WKMR
WCPB	WMPB
WCSH	WMTJ
WCTE	WMVS
WCVI	WMYA
WCWF	WOFL
WEAO	WOGX
WECT	WOIO
WEDH	WUAB
WGIQ	WUCW
WGNM	WUFT
WGPT	WWLP
WGRZ	WWPB
WGSA	
WGTQ	
WGVK	
WGXA	
WKAS	

```
J M O A P H L O W B H F C T
A L O Y Y M F R A S M E H L
X L I Z A M O A X H K L X D
H A O N S Z W H L P K K G B
K W K A S R Q M A X G W W M
V F S C E G C I T W W K T W
G G B P C W C L F J E C F N
W E T E C W C C B F A F U I
T I C T W C V I U Y W T W W
H H E C F S V M W O G X W O
C D W W T H V D Z E J L J D
U E C P G R W O I O P B V Q
Z W G I Q N K E Z P X P P Z
F W G R L W M P B A U W Q L
F Y U T K M R F T I I W N I
B A V N Q I C B H M G Y C K
```

Solution on Page 306

ALAN ALDA

ALICE

BOB NEWHART

CHER

CHINA BEACH

DEAN MARTIN

DON JOHNSON

DYNASTY

EXTRAS

FAME

FLIP WILSON

GIRLS

GLEE

HELEN HUNT

HOMELAND

I SPY

JANE WYMAN

JON HAMM

KOJAK

LEE REMICK

LOST

LOU GRANT

MAD MEN

MANNIX

NYPD BLUE

PETER FALK

REDD FOXX

RHODA

ROOTS

TAXI

THE OFFICE

THE ROGUES

THE SHIELD

TWIN PEAKS

UGLY BETTY

```
P P K A N Y P D B L U E E U
E Q O L T N A R G U O L M G
T A J A N E W Y M A N T A L
E D A N U X R P M C Y H F Y
R O K A H T T S O L T E L B
F H R L N R G I R L S S I E
A R C D E A L I C E A H P T
L E X A L S K A E P N I W T
K C I M E R E E L G Y E I Y
J I N M H B C H E R D L L M
O F N I T R A M N A E D S A
N F A O N O S N H O J N O D
H O M E L A N D I X A T N M
A E K B O B N E W H A R T E
M H X X O F D D E R C M X N
M T H E R O G U E S T O O R
```

Solution on Page 306

AUNT

BARNEY

BROMANCE

CANADIAN

COBIE SMULDERS

COLLEGE

DATING

DAVID HENRIE

ENGAGED

FRIENDSHIP

JOSH RADNOR

KIDS

LAW STUDENT

LAWYER

LILY

LYNDSY FONSECA

MARRIED

MARSHALL

NEWS

PICK UP LINE

RELATIONSHIP

ROBIN

ROMANTIC

SITCOM

SON

TED

UNCLE

WESLEYAN

WIFE

WOMANIZING

YUPPIE

```
D R P I C K U P L I N E R T
M P O R O M A N T I C S O E
Y D Y B B A R N E Y D W F L
E D A V I D H E N R I E U C
E F R I E N D S H I P N T N
D P I H S N O I T A L E R U
E R N W M K E N G A G E D W
I S O N U N A Y E L S E W O
R M O N L I L L A H S R A M
R L Y N D S Y F O N S E C A
A E G A E A Y U P P I E R N
M Z N A R B R O M A N C E I
W A I U S O N H D L I L Y Z
C U T N E D U T S W A L W I
W P A T E G E L L O C D A N
K I D S S I T C O M J S L G
```

Solution on Page 306

ALFRED NUGENT

ALLEN LEECH

AMY NUTTALL

ARISTOCRATIC

BERYL PATMORE

CARSON

CASTLE

COUNTESS

CRAWLEY

DAN STEVENS

DRAMA

EARL

ED SPELEERS

ELSIE HUGHES

ESTATE

ETHEL PARKS

GEORGE V

GRANTHAM

GWEN DAWSON

ITV

JIM CARTER

JOHN BATES

KEVIN DOYLE

LESLEY NICOL

PBS

SERVANTS

THOMAS HOWES

WORLD WAR I

```
L C J O H N B A T E S K C E
L J I M C A R T E R O R A D
A E T B E T H E L P A R K S
T L V B E A L V O W I S N P
T Y F E L M H E L S E E R E
U O N R N A A E T R V W L L
N D O Y E R Y O V E E O O E
Y N S L L D C A T S G H C E
M I R P L R N S N T R S I R
A V A A A T N U L A O A N S
H E C T S A P P G T E M Y E
T K I M D F K B N E G O E L
N C C O U N T E S S N H L T
A S I R A W D L R O W T S S
R E S E H G U H E I S L E A
G G W E N D A W S O N Z L C
```

Solution on Page 307

AWARDS

CABLE

CARTOON

CHAIR

COMEDY

COMMERCIAL

COUCH

DRAMA

DVR

FAMILY

GUIDE

HOUR

LISTINGS

MOVIE

MUSIC

MYSTERY

NETWORK

NEWS

OTTOMAN

PREMIUM

PROGRAM

REALITY

RECLINER

RECORDED

RELAX

REMOTE

SATELLITE

SCHEDULE

SERIES

SHOW

SITCOM

SNACK

SOFA

SPECIAL

SPORTS

SUSPENSE

TAPE

TELETHON

WATCH

WEATHER

```
S N A C K U N E H N R A S E
P R O G R A M C L Y E L T P
Y P R E M I U M F B L A R A
D Q C O A O P A D M A I O T
E E T O C W M F Y V X C P U
M T D E M I A S E I R E S H
O O R R L M T R N L N P I C
C S A Y O E E E D I O S T T
B U M J R C T R C S O A C A
W S A Y S W E H C T T T O W
E P R W O N A R O I R E M O
A E E R I I E H Q N A L G H
T N K L R E D I U G C L H S
H S C I S U M Q V S S I O O
E E L U D E H C S O K T U F
R E A L I T Y Y E T O M E R A
```

Solution on Page 307

AGENT

AIKIDO

BLACKLIST

BRAINS

BRUCE CAMPBELL

BURNED

CHASE

CIA

COBY BELL

DISCREDITED

EXPLOSION

FIGHT

FIONA

FLORIDA

HERO

HYPOCHONDRIAC

IRISH

JESSE

MACHINE GUN

MADELINE

MARTIAL ARTS

MIAMI

PISTOL

SAM

SHARON GLESS

SPY

SUNGLASSES

TOUGH GUY

VIOLENCE

WARRIOR

WESTEN

YOGURT

```
L P I S T O L T H G I F J P
E L G N H Q S R B U C V E S
E G E J H A T U R H O I S E
S G N B Y C R G A Y B O S S
A N I U P B A O I W Y L E S
H A L R O M L Y N P B E A A
C N E N C A A A S G E N I L
T O D E H Z I C C Q L C R G
O I A D O E T K E K L E I N
U F M N N P R S I C L C S U
G L F E D T A O A D U I H S
H O S J R I M A I M O R S G
G R N O I S O L P X E I B T
U I A M A C H I N E G U N C
Y D I S C R E D I T E D K S
W A R R I O R W E S T E N F
```

Solution on Page 307

ACC

AGGIES

BCS

BEAVERS

BIG EAST

BIG TEN

BOWL

BRUINS

BUCKEYES

BULLDOGS

CADETS

COLLEGE

DUCKS

EAGLES

ESPN

FALCONS

FOOTBALL

GATORS

HAWKEYES

HOKIES

HORNETS

HOYAS

HUSKIES

JAGUARS

JAYHAWKS

LEAGUE

MONEY

NCAA

POPULAR

REBELS

REGIONAL

REVENUE

SCHOOL

SEC

SOONERS

SPARTANS

STUDENTS

TIGERS

TROJANS

VIKINGS

```
R K R E B E L S R O T A G D
C A D E T S R E N O O S C U
E R E V E N U E A G L E S C
S B G W P O P U L A R I L K
J E S T P C S P A R T A N S
A A I C O L L E G E N P F H
G V Y G B A W B Y O S O U S
U E S H G F O I I E O S R E
A R G N A A B G Y T K E M I
R S N E A W E E B I G W C K
S N I T C R K A E I M L A O
N A K G N C L S T E N R O H
I J I I U L S T U D E N T S
U O V B U L L D O G S Q Q G
R R L E A G U E S C H O O L
B T Y E N O M S A Y O H D Z
```

Solution on Page 307

ADOLESCENCE

APARTMENT

ARTIST

BEST FRIEND

BROTHER

CARLY

CELEBRITY

CHUCK

CONTESTS

DAN SCHNEIDER

DANCING

FAME

FREDDIE

FRIENDSHIP

GIBBY

GIRL

GUARDIAN

GUPPY

KIDS

LEWBERT

LOFT

NATHAN KRESS

NEVEL

NICKELODEON

NOAH MUNCK

RECIPES

RELATIONSHIP

SAM

SEATTLE

SISTER

STAR

STUDIO

UNDERGROUND

WASHINGTON

WEB

```
P F J U N D E R G R O U N D
O R G S E A T T L E C O N A
N I E I D D E R F O A E T N
W E D D R O V A N H I P R C
A N V U I L M T M R N I E I
S D I E T E E U F A Y H B N
H S A S L S N T T R L S W G
I H P I T C S H C T R N E I
N I A S K E A H C I A O L B
G P R T B N U O Q S C I Y B
T Q T E K C L O F T N T I Y
O J M R K E N A I D R A U G
N O E D O L E K C I N L D U
H S N M Y T I R B E L E C P
S S T A R B R O T H E R H P
K I D S E P I C E R W E B Y
```

Solution on Page 308

ABC

AMERICAN IDOL

ANALOG

ANTENNA

BONANZA

BROADCAST

CAMERA

CBS

CHEERS

COLOR

CRT

DALLAS

DIGITAL

DYNASTY

FAMILY TIES

FARNSWORTH

FLAT PANEL

FRIENDS

GUNSMOKE

HAPPY DAYS

HBO

HDTV

I LOVE LUCY

LCD

LED

MINISERIES

MONITORS

MONOCHROME

NBC

PLASMA

PROGRAM

RCA

SEASONS

SEINFELD

SOUND

STAR TREK

TRANSMISSION

TUBE

VIDEO

```
D E L A Z N A N O B H X A S
A T F F K E R T R A T S T E
L D R L T E K O M S N U G I
L D I A K U A A O E D I V N
A Y E T N D B M B F S M T F
S N N P C S S E A S E O D E
Y A D A C R M R E S I N H L
A S S N E R N I B E T O A D
D T W E O S R C S A Y C N I
Y Y H L W E B A O S L H N G
P C O O S A N N U O I R E I
P C R I R A C I N N M O T T
A T N E L B R D D S A M N A
H I M O N I T O R S F E A L
M A G U Y C U L E V O L I C
C D P R O G R A M S A L P D
```

Solution on Page 308

AIM

ANGLE

BAG

BIRDIE

BOB HOPE

BUNKER

CADDY

CART

CHIP

CLUB

COURSE

DRIVE

EAGLE

FLAG

FLORIDA

FORE

FOURSOME

GLOVES

GOLFERS

GREEN

HAT

HOLE

HOOK

IRON

MAJORS

PAR

PGA TOUR

PLAYOFFS

PUTT

RAKE

REGULAR

ROUGH

SAND

SLICE

STROKE

TEE

UNIQUE

US OPEN

WEDGE

WOOD

Solution on Page

```
S X L D C X F S N S W C A P
O O T A B B L I T T A H N O
M P D F U I U E R R O I G G
U D R L C N R N T O P P L E
Y F C E I O T D K K N O E G
U D U Q F H O B I E V I R D
J E U Q C G O L F E R S Y E
H E M A J O R S S L B F F W
D N A S H P U T T O B F W N
G R E G U L A R X H O O S M
Q J U N L N D M S U B Y I B
D O O W E E I K R E H A C C
R F P E E P R S G F O L K D
A T R T R U O T A G P P A R
K G A L F M L S B T E J K V
E D G H E E F Q U M G T Z M
```

Solution on Page 308

AIRBORNE

BEN CAPLAN

BULL

CARWOOD

COMRADESHIP

COURAGE

CRAIG HEANEY

DALE DYE

DIVISION

DOUG ALLEN

EASY COMPANY

EION BAILEY

ENEMY

EXPLOSION

FRANK

GEORGE

INFANTRY

JAMES MADIO

KIRK ACEVEDO

MEDIC

PARACHUTED

RICK GOMEZ

RICK WARDEN

ROBERT

ROBIN LAING

ROY COBB

SCOTT GRIMES

SKINNY

UTAH BEACH

```
Z E M O G K C I R O B E R T
L N S I E S B Q S K I N N Y
B E E D N N E L L A G U O D
K M M A R C N K N A R F I E
I Y I M O A C R C U G F S T
R P R S B R A O R N X S O U
K I G E R W P Y A G D R L H
A H T M I O L C I N A I P C
C S T A A O A O G I L C X A
E E O J V D N B H A E K E R
V D C I D E M B E L D W G A
E A S Y C O M P A N Y A R P
D R Y R T N A F N I E R O L
O M C O U R A G E B L D E L
N O I S I V I D Y O N E G U
H C A E B H A T U R W N Y B
```

Solution on Page 308

ACTING	PLAN
BLOCK	PREMIERE
BLURB	RATING
CALENDAR	REALITY
CHOICES	RECORD
COMEDY	REMOTE
DATE	RERUN
DRAMA	SERIES
EPISODE	SHOW
EVENT	SIT
FAVORITES	SOAP
FINALE	SPECIAL
GAME	SPORTS
GUIDE	STAR
HOUR	TALK
LATEST	TIME
LENGTH	TITLE
LISTING	WATCH
MARATHON	
MOVIE	
NEW	
PILOT	

```
L I G N I T A R E C O R D C
O N B N W T O L I P F G P P
B S E R I E S T H R S E L R
Z P E W U T C A L E N D A R
J O J E N L S T T M I T N G
L R M N D U B I C I S V A Y
O T P O W O R M L E P M O S
J S J H K O S E C R E E W M
K L A T V C F I R E C Z A I
T A M A R D O I P R I H T W
N C F R C H T L N E A T C O
E T O A C T A G B A L G H H
V I J M I T I D U L L N O S
E T O M E R I N A I N E U O
F L E S P D V S G T D L R A
D E T Z K Y Y K S Y E E E P
```

Solution on Page 309

AUDIO

CAMCORDER

CAMERA

CINEMA

CLIP

DESIGN

DIGITAL

DIRECT

DOCUMENT

EDIT

EVENT

FILM

FOCUS

FOOTAGE

FRAMING

LAPTOP

LIGHTING

LOCATION

MEMORIES

MOVIE

MUSIC

PARTIES

PAUSE

PRODUCE

RECITALS

RECORD

RELEASE

SCRIPT

SHOT

SOCCER

SOFTWARE

SOUND

TAPE

TRAVEL

TRIPOD

VIDEO

WATCH

WEBCAM

WEDDING

ZOOM

```
L S O Z S E I R O M E M G S
S L C I C I N E M A H M N K
E E D R D T I D E F U E I K
T V I I I U O R O S I P T S
G A E T G P A O I V O N H T
N R P N R I T C O T E O G V
I T T E T A T M P M T I I Q
D E S I G N P A U S E T L A
D P W E P I L C L R U A T U
E R A W T F O S E W G C A N
W O T J D D A L U N M O O Z
P D C C V R E C I T A L S F
D U H I E A O M A C B E W I
R C D M S R A C S O U N D L
Z E A E W R I R E C C O S M
O C Q Z F F J D T R I P O D
```

Solution on Page 309

ACTION

ALEX

BENJAMIN

BRAD

BROTHER

CELLMATE

COP

CRIME

CROOKED

DEATH ROW

ESCAPE

FERNANDO

GANG

GRETCHEN

GUARD

JAIL

MICHAEL

MOB

MURDER

PAUL

POLITICIAN

PRISON

ROBERT KNEPPER

SERIALIZED

TATTOO

THEODORE

THRILLER

WADE WILLIAMS

WARDEN

```
V I T D T F S Z B Y P O W R
G D M U R D E R D F E L O N
V G P R I S O N E W U P R E
E I R J Q T X R Q A Z O H D
S R G E H B N E P D B L T R
T S O E T A M L L E C I A A
U E R D N C F I R W R T E W
T R T D O B H T N I O I D N
H I O G S E K E E L O C R M
R A C L K N H S N L K I A Y
I L H R E J C T T I E A U Y
L I G P I A X E L A D N G C
L Z P G P M H T J M T X V B
E E O E A I E C A S E T R M
R D C Y W N N O I T C A O J
W X M K M P G I L M D B Z O
```

Solution on Page 309

AD RATES

ADVERTISING

AGE RANGE

ANALYSIS

AUDIENCE

CALCULATED

CHANNELS

COMPOSITION

DEMOGRAPHIC

HABITS

HOME

HOUSEHOLDS

INFORMATION

MARKET

MEASUREMENT

MEDIA

MODELS

NETWORK

PERCENT

POINTS

POPULATION

PROGRAMMING

RESEARCH

SETS

SHARE

SHOW

SIZE

STATISTICS

SWEEPS

TARGET

TELEVISION

TOTAL

WATCHING

```
P T R I D E T A L U C L A C
O A E A N A L Y S I S A G H
P R S I Z F W O H S R D N A
U G E D K F O P P U H R I N
L E A E G N A R E G A A M N
A T R M E R D S M Z B T M E
T N C P G S V T H A I E A L
I E H O X G E A O K T S R S
O M M I M N R T U R S I G E
N E P N O I T I S O P M O C
D R E T D H I S E W E A R N
T U R S E C S T H T E R P E
O S C H L T I I O E W K E I
T A E A S A N C L N S E M D
A E N R J W G S D L B T O U
L M T E L E V I S I O N H A
```

Solution on Page 309

ACCENT

AMERICAN

AUTHORITY

BARBED WIRE

BOB CRANE

BOMB

BUMBLING

CAMP

CARTER

COMEDY

COVERT

DECEPTION

ESCAPE

FRONT

GERMAN

GUARD

HANS

HELMET

HOGAN

IVAN DIXON

JOHN BANNER

KINCH

KLINK

MISSION

MONOCLE

PARACHUTE

POW

RADIO

RAGTAG

RESISTANCE

ROBERT

SABOTAGE

SERGEANT

SOLDIER

SPY

STALAG

STEREOTYPE

UNIFORM

WAR

WWII

```
G K T R E V O C O M E D Y T
U N G A T G A R C A R T E R N
N I U D F N M I S S I O N P P
I L A I J I E N A R C B O B B
F K R O O L P V O N S W I S
O F D X H B Y H I O E E T T
R R S N N M T R I X R T P A
M O N A B U O E W I G U E L
O N A C A B E I W D E H C A
N T H I N O R D T N A C E G
O N O R N M E L E A N A D E
C E G E E B T O M V T R P R
L C A M R F S S L I I A M M
E C N A T S I S E R C P A A
S A B O T A G E H S P Y C N
K I N C H K T R E B O R A W
```

Solution on Page 310

ADAM SANDLER

ADELE

ADRIANA LIMA

ALEC BALDWIN

AMANDA BYNES

BEN AFFLECK

BEN STILLER

CELINE DION

CHER

ELTON JOHN

GLENN BECK

HUGH LAURIE

JEFF DUNHAM

JOHNNY DEPP

KANYE WEST

KATY PERRY

KOBE BRYANT

MADONNA

MEL GIBSON

MICHAEL BAY

RAY ROMANO

TIGER WOODS

TINA FEY

TOBY KEITH

TYLER PERRY

```
L M S O N A M O R Y A R C A
P P E D Y N N H O J W H Y N
K P N H O J N O T L E Z E N
C T Y L E R P E R R Y F F O
E S B T O B Y K E I T H A D
B E A L E C B A L D W I N A
N W D D Y A B L E A H C I M
N E N Y R R E P Y T A K T A
E Y A D E I R U A L H G U H
L N M B E N A F F L E C K N
G A A C E L I N E D I O N U
A K O B E B R Y A N T G C D
D D U B E N S T I L L E R F
E U S D O O W R E G I T G F
L M T N O S B I G L E M X E
E Q R E L D N A S M A D A J
```

Solution on Page 310

APPAREL

ARDENT

BANNER

BASEBALL

BASKETBALL

BOXING

CHEER

CLAPPING

COLLEGE

COLORFUL

DEDICATION

EAGER

FOOTBALL

GAME

GEAR

GOLF

HATS

HOCKEY

JERSEY

LOGO

LOYALTY

MASCOT

NASCAR

PENNANT

POSTER

RACING

RIVALRY

SHOUTING

SIGNS

SOCCER

SOCIAL

SUPPORT

TEAM

TENNIS

TICKETS

TRACK

UNITY

VOICE

WATCH

YELL

```
E C I O V G N I C A R X G L
O C F W O P T E N N I S E A
D S H O U T I N G U V R A I
G E W B O N R E N N A B R C
T H D A A T I Q I P L L A O
J R O I T S B T P Y R O R S
C E A C C C E A Y E Y G D P
O L R C K A H B L L O O E D
L B A S K E T B A L L Y N S
O O C P E R Y I F L T R T R
R X S E P Y E C O L L E G E
F I A N C I N C A N K G A T
U N N N H K N Y C C Q A M S
L G M A E T O G I O P E E O
V U T N E L L T O C S A M P
A S U T R O P P U S N G I S
```

Solution on Page 310

AUDIO

BRAND

CASH

CHANNELS

COLOR

COMPONENT

CONTROL

COST

DEFINITION

DELIVERY

DISPLAY

FEATURES

FLAT

HANGING

HERTZ

INCHES

INPUT

MODE

MOUNT

PICTURE

PIXELS

PLASMA

QUALITY

REMOTE

RESOLUTION

SCREEN

SHARP

SIZE

SOUND

SPEAKER

SPECIFICATIONS

STAND

SYSTEM

VIDEO

WARRANTY

```
D A F F P S T A N D C A S H
N S E R Y Z S E H C N I Z E
U F A S B Y P T A L F D L R
O H T C R T E U N Q E O O T
S E U O A N C P G F R L W Z
M N R S N U I O I T O A A A
Q W E T D O F N N C R T M R
U N S N E M I O G R T S T E
A N L E L T C T A A A U V K
L W E N I T A N U L A X R A
I Y N O V S T D P L M U V E
T S N P E Y I P I Y O O I P
Y U A M R O O Z X O V S D S
D M H O Y Z N R E M O T E E
Y T C C D I S P L A Y G O R
A I N P U T J Z S C R E E N
```

Solution on Page 310

ACTION

ADS

ARTISTIC

BLOGS

CARTOONS

CHANNEL

CLIPS

COMEDY

CUT

DIGITAL

DRAMA

EDIT

EFFECTS

EMBED

FILM

FLASH

FOLDER

FRIENDS

FUNNY

GAMING

HITS

LAPTOP

LIGHTING

MEMORIES

MOVIE

NETFLIX

NEWS

PRODUCED

PROMOTE

PUBLISH

REALITY

RECORD

SHARE

SHOOT

SPORTS

STREAM

TRAILER

TRAINING

VIRAL

WEBCAM

```
S Y D E M O C L I P S D A G
H D I S H A R E P O T P A L
O E G H I T S T R E A M M A
O C I T S I T R A G I R A R
T U T S D N L E N N A H C I
I D A D K R O I G F P J B V
D O L N F X N O D E B M E A
E R Z E L I G H T I N G W M
M P N I A M E M O R I E S A
O S E R S K P P D E A P P R
V B T F H U B R F L C C O D
I L F C B F O O O I T W R Q
E O L L E C V M L A I S T M
N G I S E F U O D R O W S L
N S X R C X F T E T N E Z I
H Q Y T I L A E R Y N N U F
```

Solution on Page 311

KAQY	KMOT
KARD	KPIC
KASN	KPLC
KATN	KPMR
KAWB	KSBI
KAZD	KSCE
KBCA	KSDK
KDKF	KUBD
KDLH	KUCW
KDMD	KUED
KDNL	KWDK
KDRV	KWET
KFQX	KWHB
KFTC	KWKB
KFVE	KWMJ
KFWD	KWOG
KITV	KWPL
KJAC	KWSD
KJCT	
KJLA	
KMEB	
KMID	

```
C Z K W S D S S N R P Z O K
J I G U M F W J L V Q D Q Y
M M E K E V W U N N E O Y G
O Q W T X D R W T T D R L L
O P B K W K Z D A C B K I F
L C D W U H F A K A S N A O
M E B H E C L A K A Q Y V K
R L U B R E W D D Z R Y S B
P I K M E B C M K M C D G K
Z N P W D V X D F T K A K B
G G I W E Q F K F Q X A J Q
T S C T L T I K F W D V U K
O O K J C T R M P K I K V J
G Z C A V L T R C X M W V L
F H K K F M P I B S K O P A
D X V T E C S K D W K G T Y
```

Solution on Page 311

ABC

BARNEY MILLER

BEWITCHED

BRADY BUNCH

BURBANK

DARK SHADOWS

DAYTIME

DISNEY

ESPN

FAMILY FEUD

FRED SILVERMAN

HAPPY DAYS

LOST

MANHATTAN

MOD SQUAD

MODERN FAMILY

NBA

NEWS

NIGHTLINE

PASSWORD

PRIMETIME

RATINGS

ROOTS

SHARK TANK

SOAP

STREAMING

TAXI

THAT GIRL

THE BACHELOR

THE TASTE

THE VIEW

THIS WEEK

```
S I R Y B G N I M A E R T S
H X J L E M I T E M I R P N
A A R I W S G N I T A R I T
R T E M I T Y A D B O G H Q
K H L A T T S A C O H E B R
T E L F C H I O T T T R K D
A B I N H E Z S L A A E A U
N A M R E V L I S D E R F E
K C Y E D I N T Y W K E T F
N H E D B E E B S S N S H Y
A E N O E W U I H L B P A L
B L R M A N H A T T A N T I
R O A L C T D I S N E Y G M
U R B H M O D S Q U A D I A
B D R O W S S A P A O S R F
N E W S Y A D Y P P A H L L
```

Solution on Page 311

BILL HAYES

BOYFRIEND

BRADY

BROTHER

DAUGHTER

DAYTIME

DEIDRE HALL

DOUG

FAMILY

FATHER

GIRLFRIEND

GOSSIP

HOPE

HOURGLASS

HUSBAND

JACK

JAMES SCOTT

JOHN

JOSH TAYLOR

KATE

KYLE LOWDER

LEXIE

LOVE

LUCAS

MAX

MOTHER

NICOLE

PATRICK

PHILIP

RUMOR

SALEM

SHAWN

SISTER

SON

STEFANO

TONY

TRIALS

VICTOR

WIFE

WILL

```
G N W A H S H O P E T A K J
P I L I H P Y N O T D O U G
K C I R T A P S A L E M O O
G O D N E I R F L R I G N J
O L O V E D P I E F D X A M
S E D E F I W T B O R M F S
S S A L G R U O H O E Z E I
I R U M O R Y R L S H Y T S
P S G N E F E Y S E A D S T
A X H H R H A C Y H L A O E
I O T I T T O L L U L Y N R
J A E O H T E L I S U T K O
F N R S T X I I M B C I C T
D B O E I B D W A A A M A C
U J R E H T O M F N S E J I
D M T R I A L S Y D A R B V
```

Solution on Page 311

AGENT

AL CAPONE

ALCOHOL

ANGELA

ARNOLD

BOARDWALK

BOOTLEGGING

BOSS

BRADY NOON

CHALKY

CHARLIE COX

CONNOR NOON

CORRUPTION

CRIME

EDDIE

ELIAS

EMILY

ENOCH

GANGSTER

GILLIAN

IMMIGRANT

IRISH

JACK HUSTON

LUCY

MARGARET

NEW JERSEY

NEW YORK

OWEN

PAUL SPARKS

POLITICIAN

RICHARD

SHERIFF

TREASURER

VETERAN

WARD

```
E N O C H K T E E M I R C Y
N D H S A I L E D T M V S K
A L S P N L P A R D M E S L
I O I A O U C C W A I T O A
L H R U O D R A W D G E B H
L O I L N O I T P U R R O C
I C C S Y O N E W O A A A W
G L H P D L O N R A N N O M
F A A A A G A N G S T E R B
F L R R R Y E S R E J W E N
I E D K B L U K R O Y W E N
R G I S E M I L Y T N E G A
E N B O O T L E G G I N G L
H A P O L I T I C I A N O U
S J A C K H U S T O N X L C
X R E R U S A E R T X A E Y
```

Solution on Page 312

ADOLESCENCE

AFFECTION

ALLEY MILLS

AMERICANA

BOY

CHILDHOOD

DAN LAURIA

DATING

DRAMEDY

EXPERIENCES

FRED SAVAGE

FRIEND

GIRL

GROWING UP

HANGS OUT

HIGH SCHOOL

HUMOR

JASON HERVEY

JUNIOR HIGH

KAREN

KEVIN

KISS

LIFE

LOVE

NORMA

NOSTALGIA

PAUL

PUBERTY

REMINISCES

STUDENT

SWEETHEART

TEEN

TRAUMAS

WINNIE

YOUNG

```
N I V E K T U O S G N A H E H
K G D S A M U A R T N I G K
L Y T R E B U P E K G A B G
N O S T A L G I A H V O I T
D S V E D M N R S A Y R N R
H L I E C N E C S E L O D A
G L T N I N H D V B I D N E
I I N W G O E R Y T K A E H
H M E E O R E I C O C T I T
R Y D L F H O E R I U I R E
O E U H N I F W R E W N F E
I L T O N F L E I O P G G W
N L S K A A M R O N M X B S
U A I R U A L N A D G U E S
J S E C S I N I M E R U H I
D O O H D L I H C L U A P K
```

Solution on Page 312

ANNOUNCER

BOWLING

BROADCAST

CHAMPIONSHIP

COMMENTARY

COMMERCIAL

CRICKET

CYCLING

DARTS

DIVING

FINALS

FISHING

GAME

GOLF

GYMNASTICS

HOCKEY

LACROSSE

MATCH

NASCAR

NCAA

OLYMPICS

PUB

RACING

RECAP

REPLAY

RESTAURANT

RUGBY

SCORE

SIDELINES

SKATING

SKIING

SOCCER

SPRINT

SWIMMING

TEAM

TENNIS

TRACK

TRIATHLON

```
C H A M P I O N S H I P U B
Y O S K A T I N G N I V I D
C D M A T C H K C A R T H S
L G A M E T S A C D A O R B
I S G R E A N N O U N C E R
N I N E T N A C M R O R P F
G N I S F S T A M U L I L L
N N C T C S P A E G H C A O
I E A A G I P A R B T K Y G
H T R U N D T R C Y A E F N
S E E R I E B S I E I T I I
I R C A M L K V A N R T N L
F O C N M I T V L N T R A W
M C O T I N S C I P M Y L O
A S S N W E H O C K E Y S B
P W G E S S O R C A L Y G J
```

Solution on Page 312

ARTIST

BILLY

BLOOD

BRENDA

BUSINESS

CALIFORNIA

CHENOWITH

CHILDHOOD

CLAIRE

COMEDY

CORPSE

DARK

DAVID

DEATH

DRUG ABUSE

EMBALMING

FAMILY

FATHER

FEDERICO

FISHER

FUNERAL

GEORGE

JEREMY SISTO

KEITH

MELODRAMA

NATE

PETER KRAUSE

POLICEMAN

REDHEAD

SECRET

SMOKING

SON

STRANGE

TEACHER

TEENAGE

VANESSA

WIDOW

```
R E H C A E T B E Z O F V W
E E C P W C X I S R T E A O
D N H L H A S L U V S D N D
H A F T A L D L B U I E E I
E T A D A I A Y A G S R S W
A E I M O F R R G E Y I S R
D E T W A O K E U O M C A E
N N E K O R H Z R R R E O G H
E A R M E N D D D G R M N S
R G C T B I E O L E E E I I
B E E P S A T H L I J D K F
P P S N B S L H C E H Y O A
V P O L I C E M A N M C M M
D S O T U B U S I N E S S I
C O R P S E L F U N E R A L
D A V I D S T R A N G E K Y
```

Solution on Page 312

ANALYSIS

ANNOUNCER

BANTER

BREAKING

CAMERAS

CAREER

CELEBRITY

COHERENT

CONCISE

DESK

DISCUSS

ENGAGING

FIELD

FLUENT

GROOMED

HEADLINE

INSIGHT

LIGHT

LIVE

LOCAL

MAKEUP

MONITOR

NEWSCAST

NOTES

PAPERS

POLISHED

REPORT

ROVING

SCREEN

SPORTS

STORY

STUDIO

SUIT

TALK

TIE

UPDATES

VIDEO

VOICE

WARNING

WEATHER

```
S E T A D P U W G N I V O R
G Y N L P A I B A N T E R E
N T E A G P D E H S I L O P
I I R C R E Z K A A U I T O
N R E O O R E C S R S G I R
R B H L O S S A C E Y H N T
A E O S M W I R R M R T O A
W L C A E S C E E A O G M L
E E E N D T N E E C T N A K
A C C A U R O R N L S I K X
T F I L T O C N I K T G E O
H I O Y K P N V L U U A U E
E E V S X S E N D X D G P D
R L E I I B R E A K I N G I
R D I S C U S S E I O E T V
T L F L U E N T H G I S N I
```

Solution on Page 313

ANIMATION

BIG LOVE

BOXING

BROADCAST

CABLE

CLASSICS

COMEDY

CRASHBOX

DEADWOOD

DOCUMENTARIES

DRAMA

ENLIGHTENED

ENTOURAGE

FAMILY

GIRLS

JOHN ADAMS

LATINO

LUCK

MOVIES

NEWSROOM

ON DEMAND

ROME

SATELLITE

SCHEDULE

SERGIO

SERIES

SHOWS

SIGNATURE

SUBSCRIPTION

TELEVISION

TREME

TRUE BLOOD

ZONE

```
L L A T I N O I T A M I N A
S E I R A T N E M U C O D M
I B I G L O V E G N I X O B
G S E R I E S N J T Q V S Z
N B E M E R T L P O I X A O
A R S N O I S I V E L E T N
T O C M K H R G S C T G E E
U A H C A C V H L R Y A L W
R D E A S D O T U A L R L S
E C D B M W A E C S I U I R
Y A U L S A B N K H M O T O
D S L E J L R E H B A T E O
E T E M O R N D M O F N K M
M D O O W D A E D X J E P U
O N D E M A N D S E R G I O
C G I R L S C I S S A L C I
```

ABBOTTS

ARROGANT

BELL

BILLIONAIRE

BROOKS

CAVORTING

CBS

CEO

COMPETITION

COSMETICS

DAYTIME

DOUG DAVIDSON

DRAMA

ERIC BRAEDEN

FOSTER

GENOA CITY

IRRESPONSIBLE

JACK

JOSHUA MORROW

KATE LINDER

MICHAEL

NICHOLAS

NIKKI

PAUL

PETER BERGMAN

RELATIONSHIPS

SAGA

SHARON

VICTOR

WIFE

WISCONSIN

YOUTH

```
J M I C H A E L Y O U T H P
A S E N I S N O C S I W G E
C C O M P E T I T I O N R T
K A T E L I N D E R I I E E
D A Y T I M E S R T A F L R
C B S V I C T O R N I B A B
N B L U A P M O O W I Z T E
D O U G D A V I D S O N I R
Q T F N U A L A N B A T O G
W T O H C L M O A G A S N M
K S S C I A P N O R A H S A
N O T B R S B R O O K S H N
J N E D E A R B C I R E I I
O L R R S A L O H C I N P K
L E R G E N O A C I T Y S K
Z I C C O S M E T I C S I I
```

Solution on Page 313

ALFREDO

BANQUET

BARGAIN

BEANS

BEEF

BREAD

CHEAP

CHICKEN

CONVENIENT

COUCH

DESSERT

DISPOSABLE

EASY

ENCHILADAS

FAST

FISH

FREEZER

FROZEN

LASAGNA

MACARONI

MEAL

NUGGETS

OVEN

PACKAGED

PASTA

PIZZA

POTATOES

PREPARED

QUICK

RAVIOLI

RICE

ROLLS

SAUCE

SPAGHETTI

STEAK

STIR

SWANSON

TRAY

TURKEY

VEGETABLE

```
K C I U Q D V D Q R M E A L
Y N S A U C E N E Z O R F A
A U E O E S G Z W D O E B Z
R G T D S T E S E L S T A Z
T G U E N E T G L A N T R I
A E R R R A A S D E L E G P
X T K F I K B A I A K U A S
D S E L C C L N S D N Q I W
A P Y A O I E A P D P N N A
E A P U H V G R O E O A E N
R G C C N N A L S R T B K S
B H N O A V T M A A A M C O
Q E C R I T S C B P T T I N
N T A O Y S A E L E O S H E
O T L N A M P G E R E A C V
F I S H S C H E A P S F K O
```

Solution on Page 313

AMPLIFIER	PRIVATE
AUDIO	PROJECTOR
BASEMENT	RECEIVER
CABLE	REMOTE
CHAIR	SATELLITE
COMFORT	SCREEN
DEN	SEATS
DIGITAL	SHOWS
DVD	SOUND
EQUIPMENT	SPEAKER
EXPENSIVE	STEREO
FAMILY	SUBWOOFER
FUN	SURROUND
HOUSE	SYSTEM
LCD	TELEVISION
LIGHTING	THEATER
MAN CAVE	VCR
MONITOR	VHS
MOVIE	
MUSIC	
PLASMA	
POPCORN	

```
S U R R O U N D I G I T A L
R T N E M E S A B R A A V S
O C L F L P V Q S I M E P H
T O I O C B O E K A S T R O
I M G O H I A P N H A O O W
N F H W F T S C C C L M J S
O O T B S A A U A O P E E A
M R I U K V M N M N R R C T
D T N S E Q U I P M E N T E
N R G P I F D R L V J D O L
U E E M O V I E I Y M A R L
O T E K D V E E F E E U C I
S A Z R A D C L I W T D V T
H E V T C E X P E N S I V E
U H E N R S P F R T Y O Y Y
S T O E R E T S L E S U O H
```

Solution on Page 314

ANGEL

BARNEY MILLER

BATMAN

BONES

COLUMBO

DEAD LIKE ME

DOCTOR WHO

DRAGON BALL

FAWLTY TOWERS

FIREFLY

FRASIER

I LOVE LUCY

LOST

MONTY PYTHON

MUPPET SHOW

PERRY MASON

QUANTUM LEAP

RED DWARF

SEINFELD

SNL

STAR TREK

THE OFFICE

THE PRISONER

THE SIMPSONS

THE SOPRANOS

THE X FILES

WONDER YEARS

```
S E L I F X E H T F P B P B
S R E W O T Y T L W A F S A
O K E R T R A T S R E N D T
R E I S A R F H N P L I R M
D E A D L I K E M E M W A A
T C O A I E Y S O R U O G N
H I B L F M C I N R T N O O
E F M D I R U M T Y N D N H
S F U L R E L P Y M A E B W
O O L E E D E S P A U R A R
P E O F F D V O Y S Q Y L O
R H C N L W O N T O Z E L T
A T P I Y A L S H N M A E C
N T H E P R I S O N E R G O
O L O S T F B O N E S S N D
S M U P P E T S H O W A A G
```

Solution on Page 314

BONANZA

BRONCO

BUCKSKIN

CHEYENNE

CUSTER

DEADWOOD

DESTRY

EMPIRE

F TROOP

FIREFLY

FRONTIER

FURY

GUNSMOKE

HONDO

KLONDIKE

KUNG FU

LANCER

LARAMIE

LAREDO

LAWMAN

MAVERICK

NICHOLS

OUTLAWS

PONDEROSA

RANGO

RAWHIDE

RED RYDER

RIVERBOAT

SARA

SHANE

SKY KING

SUGARFOOT

TATE

THE LONER

WHIPLASH

WILDSIDE

ZORRO

```
S W A L T U O R E C N A L L
F I R R A N G O F T R O O P
O L A E E K O M S N U G L O
C D S F F I A Z N A N O B N
N S K D I V T O Y R T S E D
O I Y E E R R N E R I P M E
R D K R I R E N O L E H T R
B E I S O M I F R R J O E O
E C N Z K C A V L Y F D D S
K K G F H C B R E Y Y N O A
N C I O U S U G A R F O O T
A U L D D R N B D L B H W K
M S E N N E Y E H C I O D P
W T A T E O R E D I H W A R
A E W H I P L A S H A N E T
L R U F G N U K L I N E D K
```

AGNES NIXON

AMC

BABY SWITCH

BETRAYAL

BOBBIE EAKES

DEBBI MORGAN

EILEEN HERLIE

ERICA

GREENLEE

JACOB YOUNG

JAKE

JESSE

JILL LARSON

KENDALL

MYRTLE

OPAL

PALMER

PHILADELPHIA

PINE VALLEY

PREGNANCY

REBECCA BUDIG

SHOOTING

SOAP

SOCIAL ISSUES

SUBURB

SUSAN LUCCI

TAD

TRAGEDY

WEBISODE

WEDDING

YOUNG LOVE

ZACH

```
M Y H W E B I S O D E C S J
Y D C E N O X I N S E N G A
R E T S U B U R B E E A M C
T G I D U B A C C E B E R O
L A W L S I L S G L P Y N B
E R S A E E K O N N H E A Y
I T Y P U E E A I E I L G O
C G B O S A N P D E L L R U
C N A B S K D H D R A A O N
U I B E I E A P E G D V M G
L T E T L S L A W R E E I L
N O S R A L L L I J L N B O
A O S A I H B M D A P I B V
S H E Y C C R E A K H P E E
U S J A O B A R T E I H D M
S V Z L S P R E G N A N C Y
```

Solution on Page 314

AMBER RILEY

ARTIE

BECKY

BLAINE

BURT

CHOIR

CHRIS COLFER

CLUB

COMEDY

COMPETITION

CORY MONTEITH

DARREN CRISS

DIANNA AGRON

DIRECTOR

EMMA

FINN

IAN BRENNAN

JANE LYNCH

JAYMA MAYS

KURT

LEA MICHELE

MEMBERS

MIKE

NATIONALS

NAYA RIVERA

NOAH

QUINN

RACHEL

RYAN MURPHY

SAM

SCHUESTER

SPANISH

SUE

TEACHER

TINA

WILL

```
H C N Y L E N A J R V Q H U
Q T T I N A N N E R B N A I
U S I N O I T I T E P M O C
I Y M E M B E R S F U W N L
N A I N T R U B B L A I N E
N M K O C N W L E O R L E A
A A E R Y T O D C C T L M M
T M Y G H X E M K S I B M I
I Y Y A P Z J A Y I E A A C
O A D A R R E N C R I S S H
N J E N U I H A R H O U A E
A T M N M N V I O C E C M L
L R O A N R L E H C A R X E
S U C I A E D I R E C T O R
J K F D Y H S I N A P S K T
C H O I R E T S E U H C S G
```

Solution on Page 315

BAT

BRAVES

BULLPEN

BUNT

CABLE

CHEER

CLEATS

CROWD

CUBS

DIAMOND

DODGERS

FANS

FIELD

GIANTS

GLOVE

HIT

HOTDOG

INNING

LEAGUE

MLB

OUT

PEANUTS

PENNANT

PIRATES

PITCH

RECORD

REDS

RUN

SEASON

SERIES

SLIDER

SLUGGER

STRIKE

TAG

TEAM

THROW

TRIPLE

UMPIRE

UNIFORM

WALK

```
J F S I U R M D A A R Q P W
L P E K I R T S C P Y N S S
T R I P L E E S L I D E R B
N I R S L U G G E R I P M U
P O E P G T N S A A U T Y C
B A S A E D I T T T B B A H
S L E A R N N U S E U B X E
R L M B E Q N N B S L U J E
D W O R C S I A R E L N R R
N E W A O U T E N L P T U E
E U O V R F G P N T E H X D
J E R E D D I A M O N D W S
G V H S O S T N A I G L B I
H O T D O G N X U J H E X I
K L A W K O E A H C T I P N
K G A T L S N S F Z A F T S
```

Solution on Page 315

ABC NEWS

ACHIEVEMENT

ANNUALLY

BBC

BLEAK HOUSE

BOARD

CBS NEWS

CEREMONY

CNN

COMMITTEES

DOCUMENTARY

EDUCATION

EXCELLENCE

FOX

GOOD EATS

HBO SPORTS

HOMELAND

INDIVIDUALS

JUSTIFIED

LOUIE

NBC

NETWORKS

NIGHTLINE

NOVA

PBS

PORTLANDIA

QUALITY

SOUTH PARK

STANDARDS

THE OFFICE

THE SHIELD

TNT

WINNERS

YEAR

```
A S E N I L T H G I N O V A
N R I S T A N D A R D S Z N
N E U B D L E I H S E H T B
U N O P E D U C A T I O N C
A N L E C N E L L E C X E D
L I N D I V I D U A L S M E
L W F S W E N S B C U O E I
Y R A T N E M U C O D U V F
N D N A L E M O H M D T E I
O N E T W O R K S M R H I T
M P O R T L A N D I A P H S
E G O O D E A T S T O A C U
R Y T I L A U Q N T B R A J
E A A B C N E W S E N K C C
C F E E C I F F O E H T B N
X O F Y S T R O P S O B H N
```

Solution on Page 315

ACCELERATOR

ADMIRAL

AL CALAVICCI

AMNESIA

ASTRONAUT

BODY SWAP

CIGAR

COMEDY

COMPUTER

DEAN STOCKWELL

DEBORAH PRATT

DRAMA

EXPERIMENT

FUTURE

GENIUS

GOOSHIE

GOVERNMENT

HERO

HYPERSPACE

IDENTITY

LABORATORY

NBC

NOSTALGIA

PHYSICS

PROGRAMMER

REPORTER

SAM BECKETT

SCOTT BAKULA

TIME

ZIGGY

Solution on Page

```
P A W S Y D O B S U I N E G
N O S T A L G I A M A R D J
H E R O G O V E R N M E N T
G D E B O R A H P R A T T R
Y T I T N E D I E N A D R T
R E T R O P E R S L A E Z N
O A F E O R E T U P M O C E
T D U X K T O K P M K A C M
A M T A L C A L A V I C C I
R I U Q K B E R G S C R P R
O R R W T I G B E O P A H E
B A E T H O Z N M L R G Y P
A L O S R I M E I A E I S X
L C O P G A D Y T T S C I E
S O B G H Y P E R S P A C E
G U Y N U T U A N O R T S A
```

Solution on Page 315

AARON PAUL

ANNA GUNN

BETSY BRANDT

BOB ODENKIRK

BRYAN CRANSTON

CANCER

CEREBRAL PALSY

CHEMISTRY

CRIME

CRYSTAL METH

DEA AGENT

DEAN NORRIS

DIAGNOSIS

DRUG

GUSTAVO

HANK

JESSE

MANUFACTURING

MARIE

MIKE

MURDER

NEW MEXICO

PARTNERSHIP

RJ MITTE

SAUL

SCIENCE

SELLING

SKYLER

STEVEN

STUDENT

WALTER

```
E G C D S E L L I N G U R D
K U H I K L U A S T E V E N
I S E A Y D A P I N M O T K
M T M G L Y P C R E I G L U
H A I N E S N A R G R N A N
Y V S O R L O N O A C I W E
N O T S N A R C N A Y R B W
M A R I E P A E N E Z U D M
W Y Y S N L A R A D G T S E
C R Y S T A L M E T H C T X
M U R D E R H M D A Z A U I
B E T S Y B R A N D T F D C
B O B O D E N K I R K U E O
J E S S E R N N U G A N N A
P A R T N E R S H I P A T Y
E C N E I C S E T T I M J R
```

Solution on Page 316

ALIVE

AMC

ANDREA

APOCALYPSE

ATLANTA

AWAKEN

CAESAR

CARL

CHANDLER RIGGS

COMA

DALE

DANAI GURIRA

DEAD

DEPUTY

EMILY KINNEY

GEORGIA

GLENN

GREENE

GRIMES

HERSHEL

HORROR

LAUREN COHAN

LAURIE HOLDEN

LORI

MAGGIE

MERLE

MICHONNE

NORMAN REEDUS

OFFICER

RICK

SCOTT WILSON

SHANE

SHERIFF

STEVEN YEUN

SURVIVAL

THE

WALKERS

ZOMBIES

```
G C A E S A R E C I F F O V
L S E M I R G F F I R E H S
E Z Z O M B I E S B S D E E
E N E S P Y L A C O P A T R U
N E M I L Y K I N N E Y S S
O E A T N A L T A S S T H C
H N D M A G G I E T R U E O
C E A L H E G H K E E P L T
I E L O O U T C L V K E R T
M R E R R H I R I E L D A W
S G G I R R E L D N A H C I
W I R C O M A I D Y W C X L
A A N O R M A N R E E D U S
I N A H O C N E R U A L C O
N E K A W A E R D N A D M N
E N A H S U R V I V A L A H
```

Solution on Page 316

BEARS

BENGALS

BILLS

BRONCOS

BROWNS

BUCCANEERS

CARDINALS

CHARGERS

CHIEFS

COLTS

COWBOYS

DOLPHINS

EAGLES

FALCONS

GIANTS

JAGUARS

JETS

LIONS

PACKERS

PANTHERS

PATRIOTS

RAIDERS

RAMS

RAVENS

REDSKINS

SAINTS

SEAHAWKS

STEELERS

TITANS

VIKINGS

144

```
R A M S T N I A S N A T I T
C O L T S N O I L A G E Q Z
R B R O W N S S N O C L A F
C L V I S T E E L E R S O G
I K D R I A S N E V A R B I
B Z C T H T S N W A P A B A
I T P A N T H E R S A U E N
L C W P R S F E I H C G N T
L K S R E D I A R C K A G S
S S G N I K I V A I E J A O
V D O L P H I N S O R E L C
I W E A G L E S A G S T S N
C H A R G E R S F L X S E O
Q B E A R S S N I K S D E R
I B F S Y O B W O C G A E B
D V U T K Q R J X X I C F U
```

Solution on Page 316

ALF

AMEN

BATMAN

BEWITCHED

BONANZA

CHEERS

COACH

COSBY

DRAGNET

ELLEN

EMPTY NEST

EVENING SHADE

FAMILY TIES

FULL HOUSE

HAPPY DAYS

I LOVE LUCY

LIFE GOES ON

MAJOR DAD

MIAMI VICE

MISTER ED

MOONLIGHTING

MURPHY BROWN

QUANTUM LEAP

RHODA

STEP BY STEP

THAT GIRL

THE FUGITIVE

THE MUNSTERS

THE NANNY

WINGS

```
D E R E T S I M O I I L E E
B G H E F A M I L Y T I E S
W H N C B O N A N Z A F N U
I X Q I A A M E N L S E W O
N S U V T O D V F R V G O H
G Y A I M H C I E E L O R L
S A N M A T G T N R D E B L
T D T A N E S I I Y A S Y U
E Y U I F N N G L N D O H F
P P M M U G T U O N R N P Z
B P L M S A S F V A O Y R W
Y A E H H R A E E N J O U C
S H A T E D L H L E A A M O
T D P E O L N T U H M J X S
E C H H E D E H C T I W E B
P C R N T S E N Y T P M E Y
```

Solution on Page 316

ABA	LAKERS
ASSIST	LEAGUE
BASKET	NBA
BULLS	NET
CELTICS	PASS
CENTER	PLAY
COACH	POINT
COURT	RIM
DRAFT	ROUND
DUNK	RUN
EAST	SCORE
FANS	SCREEN
FINALS	SPURS
FOUL	STREET
GAME	SUNS
GUARD	TEAM
HALF	TIME
HAWKS	WEST
HOOP	
INDOOR	
JORDAN	
JUMP	

```
O H J U M P H C E N T E R O
G P C O A C H S R E K A L T
T C O U R T A R K O T E N X
Z Y L U F D G S T R E E T W
R D A T W D A D S S M F A P
M Y R H H B M N R I A B A M
Z H E K U O E U T R S T V G
C Y U H O O P O D C C T H C
Z N N W U S R R I R D H V R
P J C W E S T T B N A L D U
Z L P B U L L S H W D U I N
L E A G U E N A K A N O G E
N B S Y C A L S N K M F O E
N G S U F F K T N I O P G R
L F T N N I H G R Y F F Z C
A Z O Z O S T S A E R O C S
```

Solution on Page 317

BIG APPLE

BLUE BLOODS

BONES

CASTLE

COLD CASE

COLUMBO

DRAGNET

DUE SOUTH

EUREKA

FOREVER KNIGHT

KEEN EDDIE

KOJAK

LIE TO ME

LIFE

MATT HOUSTON

MIAMI VICE

MONK

MURDER ONE

NASH BRIDGES

NCIS

PETER GUNN

PSYCH

THE CLOSER

THE COMMISH

THE INSIDE

THE KILLING

THE MENTALIST

THE SHIELD

WHITE COLLAR

WISEGUY

```
C A S T L E N O R E D R U M
O B M U L O C O L D C A S E
N C I S D O O L B E U L B E
T O A C T H E S H I E L D I
I R S M L I E T O M E N O U D
E D I S N I E H T A U C E D
S R V L Y U G E S I W E S E
O A I M A T T H O U S T O N
L G C O P T B O N E S I U E
C N E N K R N P S Y C H T E
E E A K I A K E R U E W H K
H T U D H S I M M O C E H T
T H G I N K R E V E R O F C
L E G N I L L I K E H T Y O
S L I F E N N U G R E T E P
K O J A K B I G A P P L E G
```

Solution on Page 317

ANGEL

BABES

BLOSSOM

BOB

BRIMSTONE

CHARMED

COSBY

CUPID

CYBILL

DAMON

DREAM ON

DWEEBS

ELVIS

EXTRA

FELICITY

FRIENDS

GRAND

JENNY

JESSE

LATELINE

MADTV

MARTIN

MUSCLE

NORM

PARTNERS

PHENOM

POPULAR

PREY

ROC

SEINFELD

SIBS

SLIDERS

SPAWN

STUDS

THE CREW

THE EDGE

THE PJS

TRIBECA

WINGS

WORKING

```
S W Y E R P E W C U P I D Y
B O B M U S C L E D K F E B
I M F P O P U L A R A R M S
S D A M O N A E S E C I R O
N W O R K I N G N A E E A C
F L S N T I N O C M B N H Q
C E D F L I T C S O I D C T
G G U E W S N Y P N R S C H
Z N T L M E E B A E T S O E
P A S I R G B I W H N R S P
L Q R C O D G L N P R E E J
G B G I N E V L E F T D B S
P A R T N E R S S H E I A I
I H A Y P H M O S S O L B V
Y N N E J T D W E E B S D L
M A D T V O C G J A R T X E
```

Solution on Page 317

ACE	OUT
ADVANTAGE	OVERHAND
ARTHUR ASHE	OVERHEAD
AUDIENCE	PLAY
BALL	POINT
BILL TILDEN	QUALIFIER
CARVE	RECEIVER
CHAIR	REFEREE
CLAY	RETURN
DAVIS CUP	ROD LAVER
DEUCE	SCORE
DINK	SET
DON BUDGE	SLAM
DROP SHOT	SLICE
FAULT	SMASH
FOREHAND	SPIN
GAME	STROKE
HIT	US OPEN
LET	
LOB	
MATCH	
NET	

```
W D T J D N A H E R O F L S
X I D N A H R E V O T E L T
H N E D L I T L L I B A F E
E K O R T S H C C V M U V S
L O B P E D U R E F E R E E
R V A B U V R G R I A H C R
I E D U F C A O A C K G U O
O R C O D T S L P M J O E C
U H Y E N I H I D S E U D S
T E N A I B E N V O H S M M
L A V P L V U N P A R O A A
U D S L I C E D C O D P T S
A L N R U T E R G E I E C H
F L Q U A L I F I E R N H P
Y A L P I Q F L C M A S T W
V B Z S C H L A D S P I N A
```

Solution on Page 317

ALEX

ARIEL WINTER

BABY

BIG KID

BOY

CAT

CLAIRE

COMEDY

CULTURE

DAUGHTER

DOG

DUNPHY

FAMILY

FATHER

GIRL

GLORIA

HAPPY

HUSBAND

INTERRACIAL

JAY

LILY

LUKE

MANNY

MARRIAGE

MITCHELL

MOTHER

NOLAN GOULD

PARENTS

PHIL

PRITCHETT

RELATIONSHIP

RICO RODRIGUEZ

SARAH HYLAND

SON

TEEN

TY BURRELL

UNCONVENTIONAL

VICTORIES

WIFE

MODERN FAMILY

```
T C E G A I R R A M R T L M
Y A R I E L W I N T E R I L
O D C P R I T C H E T T H C
B R E L A T I O N S H I P L
M D F M S E I R O T C I V A
I N A A O G L O R I A F T I
T A M N N C C D E K U L D R
C L I N T E R R A C I A L E
H Y L Y B A B I G K I D U T
E H Y P P A H G E F I W O H
L H E R U T L U C L R I G G
L A N O I T N E V N O C N U
I R E H T A F Z X J A Y A A
L A B R T Y B U R R E L L D
Y S T N E R A P R E H T O M
D U N P H Y W H U S B A N D
```

Solution on Page 318

ABC	NIPKOW
ANTENNA	PATENT
BAIRD	PHILCO
BRAUN	PROGRAMMING
BROADCAST	RCA
CAMERA	REGULATION
CATHODE	REPRODUCE
CBS	SATELLITE
CHANNELS	SCAN
CRUDE	SILHOUETTE
DISPLAY	STATIONS
ELECTRONIC	TRANSMIT
ENGINEERS	TUBES
FARNSWORTH	UHF
FCC	VHF
IMAGE	WESTINGHOUSE
INVENTORS	
JENKINS	
LICENSED	
MICROWAVE	
NBC	
NETWORK	

```
D R I A B S T A T I O N S A
I E I P T S A C D A O R B E
S V S T R A N S M I T C E T
P A Z U S S R O T N E V N I
L W P R O G R A M M I N G L
A O X F V H L C P E S S I L
Y R P H A U G H A L T I N E
C C F A G R I N E E U L E T
R I A E T L N N I C B H E A
U M R W C E N S B T E O R S
D A E O T A N N W R S U S N
E G M N H C A T H O D E F I
C E A C W O K P I N R T W K
B C C D E S N E C I L T F N
S C R E P R O D U C E E H E
K R O W T E N U A R B L U J
```

Solution on Page 318

ALPHAS

AWAKE

BENT

BONES

CLERKS

CULT

DEXTER

DIRT

EXTRAS

FIREFLY

FRINGE

GIRLS

GLEE

GRIMM

HEX

HUFF

HUNG

JERICHO

JOEY

LOST

LOUIE

MAD

MEDIUM

MENTAL

MISSING

MONK

NIKITA

PSYCH

REAPER

REVENGE

ROB

SCRUBS

SKINS

SMITH

SURFACE

TITUS

TREMORS

VEGAS

WEEDS

WHITNEY

```
F O Q C H J J O P T L O S T
T A U B X I S A S K R E L C
A L E E L G R R L X I E R T
T P U G R O O M A D E E I T
I H B N B M U Z T G A H G N
Y A F I E J L I N P T S R R
G S U R F A C E E I A M G J
K B T F J X V R M R K M T K
W U D Q E E M S T P K I I E
D R A M R U F X V S D R T K
I C W F I R E F L Y E G U A
R S E D C S K S U C X N S W
T N E B H N S N B H T Y O A
A M D V O W H I T N E Y B B
U Y S M V P A K N O R X W V
A G I V E G A S J G N U H B
```

Solution on Page 318

BEAT

BRIT HUME

BUSINESS

CNN

CONTENT

CRONKITE

CYCLE

DAN RATHER

DEBATES

EDITORS

EVENTS

FORECAST

FORMAT

HARD NEWS

HUMOROUS

INTERVIEWS

JEFF GLOR

JOURNALIST

MEDIA

NETWORKS

NEWSCAST

OPINIONS

POLITICS

PUNDITS

REPORTS

RESEARCH

SPORTS

STUDIO

TECHNOLOGY

TED KOPPEL

TOM BROKAW

TRIAL

WEATHER

```
S S N O I N I P O I D U T S
T A E B Z N E W S C A S T Y
N P S F J O U R N A L I S T
E K Y W O I S E Z V J W A E
V S L G E R E H T A E W C D
E E E R O N M T B I F A E K
B T M T E L D A V D F K R O
G U I U A S O R T E G O O P
Q D S K H B E N A M L R F P
E R C I N T E A H H O B C E
A O W N N O I D R C R M O L
Q Y C I H E R R I C E O N A
P U N D I T S C B L H T T I
H U M O R O U S T R O P E R
C Y C L E S K R O W T E N T
W P O L I T I C S P O R T S
```

Solution on Page 318

ACCUSATION

ALAN CUMMING

ATTORNEY

BOSS

BROTHER

CARY

CHICAGO

CHRIS NOTH

COOK COUNTY

CORRUPTION

COURTROOM

COWORKER

DAUGHTER

DEFENSE

DIANE

ELI

FAMILY

GRACE

HUSBAND

INVESTIGATION

JACKIE

JOSH CHARLES

LAW FIRM

LAWYER

LEGAL

MAKENZIE VEGA

MATT CZUCHRY

PETER

SCHEMING

SON

TRIAL

WIFE

WILL

WORKING MOM

ZACH

```
J A C K I E M D E F E N S E
R E N O S N O A Y L I M A F
H C C M E A M U I M C A R Y
L E G A L I G G L A W Y E R
G C N T R D N H X K Y E D C
N O I T A G I T S E V N I O
I O M C H R K E O N C R C R
M K M Z C E R R G Z H O O R
E C U U H K O L A I R T U U
H O C C S R W L C E I T R P
C U N H O O A I I V S A T T
S N A R J W B W H E N E R I
H T L Y F O B O C G O F O O
C Y A I A C C U S A T I O N
A E R E H T O R B S H W M Z
Z M D N A B S U H R E T E P
```

Solution on Page 319

ACTORS	QUOTES
BEATLES	RERUNS
CABLE	RETRO
CARTOONS	SCANDAL
CHANNEL	SCENE
CLASSIC	SERIES
CLIP	SITCOMS
COMEDY	SIXTIES
DIANA	SOAPS
DRAMA	SONGS
EIGHTIES	SPECIAL
FAMILY	SPORTS
FIFTIES	STARS
FINALE	STORIES
HISTORY	THEME
KENNEDY	VARIETY
MUSIC	VIDEOS
MYSTERY	WESTERN
NEWS	
OSCARS	
PARADES	
PLOT	

Solution on Page

```
S T F S E T O U Q Y U N M U G
G S E I R E S T R O P S Y Z
N D I A N A Y Q S O E D I V
O U T M D A C T X O E A N S
S C A N D A L S E M F R T N
S E I T H G I E O I E O O U
N C L A S S I C F T R Y L R
O A E T Y R O T S I H A P E
O B N Q A K I E E P G O V R
T L N S N E W S N A Y R E F
R E A E S N B T S R O T C A
A S H I O N M S E A I E D M
C T C T A E U T C D M R R I
L A P X P D S S P E C I A L
I R X I S Y I Y H S N H M Y
P S O S M O C T I S O E A I
```

ACCESS

ANALOG

AUDIENCE

BASIC

BILLING

BRAVO

CARTOONS

CHANNEL

CHILDREN

CINEMAX

COST

DIGITAL

DOWNLINK

ESPN

GUIDE

HBO

HGTV

HISTORY

LIFETIME

LOCAL

MOVIE

MTV

NETWORK

NEWS

PACKAGE

PREMIUM

RATING

RECEIVER

REMOTE

SERIES

SHOPPING

SHOWTIME

SPORTS

STARZ

SYFY

TBS

THE CW

TLC

TNT

WATCH

```
Q Q S H I S T O R Y O B D V
C E B K N X A M E N I C U M
I O S S K K P A C K A G E U
S V E E N R R C E L A X J I
A A R I I O C O I O U Z C M
B R I V L W O S V C D H H E
M B E O N T E T E A I H A R
G A S M W E M M R L E G N P
N C P S O N I T D A N T N T
I C N B D T T R V I C V E X
T E H T W S E K L E E T L C
A S L O P N F L A T I G I D
R S H O P P I N G O L A N A
W S R Z Z B L G U I D E T Q
N T H E C W A T C H W Q N O
S T A R Z P C E M S Y F Y S
```

Solution on Page 319

ALEC BALDWIN

BERNIE MAC

BOB CRANE

BOB NEWHART

BRIAN KEITH

BURT REYNOLDS

CHARLIE SHEEN

DON CHEADLE

FRED SAVAGE

HAL LINDEN

JACK KLUGMAN

JIM PARSONS

JOHN GOODMAN

JOHN LITHGOW

JON CRYER

JUDD HIRSCH

LARRY STORCH

LEE PACE

LLOYD HAYNES

MATT LEBLANC

RAY ROMANO

STEVE CARELL

TONY RANDALL

Solution on Page 319

```
W B S T E V E C A R E L L E
Q P U L L A D N A R Y N O T
S H C R O T S Y R R A L H R
W O G H T I L N H O J E D A
J I M P A R S O N S J C C H
B R I A N K E I T H A A H W
D C J O N C R Y E R C P A E
O R A Y R O M A N O K E R N
N E D N I L L A H O K E L B
C S E N Y A H D Y O L L I O
H C S R I H D D U J U D E B
E Q F R E D S A V A G E S C
A C A M E I N R E B M V H R
D J O H N G O O D M A N E A
L M A T T L E B L A N C E N
E X A L E C B A L D W I N E
```

Solution on Page 319

ALF

AMEN

AT EASE

AUTOMAN

BOOKER

BULLSEYE

CODE RED

CONDO

DARKROOM

DAY BY DAY

DEAR JOHN

DREAMS

DUET

DYNASTY

EMPTY NEST

FRIDAYS

FULL HOUSE

HEATHCLIFF

HOMETOWN

HOOPERMAN

HOTEL

HUNTER

LOVING

MATLOCK

MIAMI VICE

MONSTERS

OPEN HOUSE

OUR HOUSE

ROSEANNE

STARMAN

STINGRAY

TEXAS

THE COLBYS

WEBSTER

WEREWOLF

```
H O M E T O W N Y D L D N H
H P M H F M G E S A E T A C
O E I U U A N M R R T Y M F
O N A N L T I A E K O T R L
P H M T L L V D T R H S A O
E O I E H O O F S O H A T W
R U V R O C L F N O N N S E
M S I T U K L R O M H Y T R
A E C H S T C I M N O D I E
N Y E E E E O D F V J G N W
A E D C T X N A L F R N G E
M S R O Y A D Y B Y A D R B
O L E L T S O S T E E U A S
T L A B U I F H S P D E Y T
U U M Y R E K O O B M T O E
A B S S O U R H O U S E I R
```

Solution on Page 320

ANN BIDERMAN

ARIJA BAREIKIS

ARREST

AUTHENTIC

BEN

CALIFORNIA

CHICKIE

COP

CRIME

DETECTIVE

DEWEY

DORIAN MISSICK

ENSEMBLE CAST

JOHN

LAPD

LOS ANGELES

LYDIA

MOTHER

NBC

OFFICER

PATROL

POLICE

RAW

REGINA KING

ROOKIE

SAL

SHAWN HATOSY

TERRY

THRILLER

TNT

WOMAN

174

```
A I D Y L K I P E M I R C Y
T R E L L I R H T I J O H N
G N I K A N I G E R Y E I B
M A T J S O D I E E N R C C
D O R I A N M I S S I C K X
N P Y R L B K T E R R Y I T
B A N T E O A M B Y S Y E M
A T M F O S B R E C I F F O
U R X R W L T W E A A A C T
T O T D E T E C T I V E M H
H L F C B D P A L O K C O E
E I A C A L I F O R N I A R
N S L R I N E B A H G L S A
T Q P S E L E G N A S O L W
I O J O Y W O M A N G P F S
C D Y S O T A H N W A H S Z
```

Solution on Page 320

ALTON BROWN

AUDIENCE

AWARDS

CELEBRITY

CHEF

CHOPPED

COOKS

CUISINES

CUPCAKE WARS

DISHES

EDUCATIONAL

EMERIL LIVE

ENDORSEMENTS

ENTERTAINMENT

FOOD

FOREIGN

FRUGAL GOURMET

GENRE

GOOD EATS

GRAHAM KERR

HOST

INFORM

INSPIRATION

JULIA CHILD

MARTHA

MEALS

PREPARE

STAGES

TEACHING

TELEVISION

VIEWERS

176

```
N G N I H C A E T D O O F T
N G O O D E A T S I N Y E L
D L I H C A I L U J P L A C
E N T E R T A I N M E N T O
P T A A R E M G R V O E E O
P C R U M O E O I I M N V K
O U I D I N F S T R D W I S
H P P I R N I A U O P O L E
C C S E I O C O R S R R L N
D A N N N U G S E F E B I I
I K I C D L E G C E P N R S
S E X E A M A R T H A O E I
H W Y G E T S O H C R T M U
E A U N S Y T I R B R E L E C
S R T Z R R E K M A H A R G
F S R E W E I V S D R A W A
```

Solution on Page 320

BLONDIE

DRAGNET

GUIDING LIGHT

HIGHWAY PATROL

I LOVE LUCY

I MARRIED JOAN

LASSIE

LAWMAN

LAWRENCE WELK

LONE RANGER

LOONEY TUNES

MISTER ED

PETER GUNN

RED SKELTON

ROY ROGERS

SEA HUNT

THE GOLDBERGS

THE GUMBY SHOW

THE RIFLEMAN

TODAY SHOW

TOM AND JERRY

TWILIGHT ZONE

WAGON TRAIN

ZORRO

```
L T G U I D I N G L I G H T
O Q H N E I D N O L B I Z H
O S R E G O R Y O R G M K E
N T W L G J O V D H R A L R
E S E A E U E R W U E R E I
Y G M O G L M A R R N R W F
T R U I U O Y B N O O I E L
U E R C S P N N Y T Z E C E
N B Y E A T U T N S T D N M
E D C T J G E U R J H J E A
S L R H R D H R J A G O R N
L O N E R A N G E R I A W A
L G T T E N G A R D L N A M
U E I S S A L G M B I N L W
P H T O D A Y S H O W R X A
K T Y R E D S K E L T O N L
```

Solution on Page 320

ABIGAIL HAWK

BROTHER

CHIEF

COP

DANNY

DAUGHTER

DETECTIVE

DINNER

ERIN

FAMILY

FATHER

FRANK

GARRETT

GREGORY JBARA

HENRY

IRISH

JACK

JAMIE

LEN CARIOU

LINDA

NEW YORK

NICKY

NYPD

POLICE

RELATIONSHIP

RETIRED

SAMI GAYLE

SEAN

SISTER

SON

TOM SELLECK

WILL ESTES

```
D A N N Y R N E H R B O O E
A D F H C K C O P Z R U A I
U N P A L G C O P S O N N M
G X I T M L L I W A T D G A
H V H T O I E I N B H R V J
T R S S C M L N N I E V S S
E W N E I L S Y C G R A N I
R V O N E R P E O A M D D S
K V I S E D I R L I R N T T
X C T T A W Y M G L D I W E
S E A N C J Y A M H E L O R
S I L J B E Y O E A R C E U
P B E A E L T J R W I H K N
G A R R E T T E N K T H U C
F A I R E N N I D A E Y L E
S N W Q C H I E F F R A N K
```

Solution on Page 321

AARON ASHMORE

AGENT

ALCOHOLIC

ARTIE

ATF

CLAUDIA

CODE BREAKER

COMPUTER

COOKIES

COVERT

GADGETS

GOVERNMENT

INTELLIGENCE

IRENE

JANE ESPENSON

JOANNE KELLY

KNOWLEDGE

LEENA

MISSING

MYKA

PARANORMAL

PETE

REGENTS

SAUL RUBINEK

SCIENCE

SEARCH

SECRET SERVICE

SOUTH DAKOTA

STEVE

SYFY

WAREHOUSE

182

```
E G D E L W O N K Q G A S K
S C I L O H O C L A O A T F
U M I S S I N G A X V R E T
O D E V S C I E N C E O V A
H J S C R I U R E T R N E G
E N O S N E P S E E N A J E
R W U A A E S P L N M S C N
A P T C N U G T D U E H O T
W H H O L N L I E H N M O R
S C D M S A E R L R T O K E
T R A P Y E U K U L C R I V
N A K U F K I D E B E E E O
E E O T Y S A T I L I T S C
G S T E G D A G R A L N N S
E P A R A N O R M A L Y E I
R E K A E R B E D O C Y G K
```

Solution on Page 321

ALAN ALDA

BEA ARTHUR

BETTY WHITE

BILL COSBY

CARL BETZ

CAROL KANE

DANA DELANY

EDIE FALCO

FRASIER

FRIENDS

GUNSMOKE

HELEN HUNT

I LOVE LUCY

JANE CURTIN

JIM PARSONS

JOHN RITTER

JUDD HIRSCH

LOST

MAD MEN

PETER FALK

RAY ROMANO

ROOTS

SOUTH PARK

STUDIO ONE

TAXI

THE MONKEES

THE WALTONS

TINA FEY

184

```
F M X B I L L C O S B Y E F
N A P J E D I E F A L C O R
V D E A B E A A R T H U R I
A M T N U H N E L E H L L E
R E E E T I H W Y T T E B N
A N R C Y E F A N I T V S D
Y O F U J I M P A R S O N S
R O A R U G A P L E C L O E
O I L T D U L C E T A I T E
M D K I D N A W D T R F L K
A U Z N H S N R A I L R A N
N T A X I M A J N R B A W O
O S C A R O L K A N E S E M
R O O T S K D N D H T I H E
D L N C C E A Q P O Z E T H
S O U T H P A R K J E R J T
```

Solution on Page 321

AFFECTION

ASHLEY OLSEN

BECKY

BOB SAGET

BROWN HAIR

BRUNETTE

CALIFORNIA

CHILDREN

CLEANING

COMEDY

DAUGHTER

DAVE COULIER

FAN

FRIEND

GIRL

GREEK

HOUSE

HUMOR

IMMATURITY

JESSE

JOEY

JOHN STAMOS

LAUGH TRACK

LOSS

MICHELLE

MOTHER

MUSICIAN

NERD

PARENT

SINGLE

SISTER

SITCOM

TWIN ACTORS

UNCLE

WIDOWER

WISECRACK

```
G R N A I C I S U M V J Y W
R E H T O M I F R I E N D B
E W W G P T D A U G H T E R
E O R Z C P S I S T E R M U
K D O O D A F F E C T I O N
K I M M A T U R I T Y A C E
C W U T V N E R D L I H C T
A S H L E Y O L S E N N Y T
R I J O C G B E C K Y W Y E
T N O S O M A T S N H O J L
H G E S U O H S N A F R E L
G L Y E L C N U B E J B S E
U E T W I N A C T O R S S H
A W I S E C R A C K B A E C
L A I N R O F I L A C H P I
J G N I N A E L C L R I G M
```

Solution on Page 321

ANCIENT

ARRYN

ARYA

BRAN

BRIENNE

CATELYN

DAENERYS

DARK

EVIL

FAMILY

FIGHT

GENDRY

GRAND

GRENN

HODOR

IRRI

JAIME

JEOR

JON

KING

LORD

MAESTER

NOBLE

OSHA

PETYR

PLOT

POWER

QUEEN

ROS

RULING

SAMWELL

SANSA

SER

STARK

THEON

TULLY

TYRELL

TYRION

TYWIN

WAR

```
K R U G F X K C S A N S A L
B W W B N T S G N E A I T O
J E O R O D Q S E Y V Y N R
I R R I B G Y U N N R I R D
C E Q E L R Q X Y I D R L A
S S A N E J D L O N V R A R
K S A N C I E N T N D O Y K
V F E E R T P C A E L D E R
W A R M A E S T E R U O M F
D M N C N H W A P G G H I J
T I Q O N S S O M Z G G A J
L L J A E I T O P W H N J I
K Y R B T H W A G T E I I C
T B Y L L U T Y R E L L C K
R V Q W Y O V D T K E U L L
X U Z T T O L P E T Y R O S
```

Solution on Page 322

ADVICE

ALEX

ANDREW

ARCHITECT

BRIAN BONSALL

BROTHER

CHILDREN

COLUMBUS

CRUSH

DAUGHTER

ELLEN

ELYSE

FAMILY

FATHER

FLASHBACKS

GRADUATE

GREED

HIPPIE

HUSBAND

JENNIFER

KEATON

LAUGH

LIBERAL

MALLORY

MARRIAGE

MOTHER

NEIGHBOR

NICK

OHIO

REPUBLICAN

SISTER

SITCOM

SKIPPY

SON

STEVEN

TIE

VALUES

VIEWPOINTS

WIFE

YOUNG

```
S F A M I L Y E F I W Q Y J
T L L A S N O B N A I R B P
N A C I L B U P E R T I E H
I S E L Y S E I P P I H R S
O H U S B A N D R E W L E U
P B E R E F I N N E J A H R
W A R C H I T E C T D R T C
E C X D M A R R I A G E O A
I K R E A D N E L L E B M W
V S C O L U M B U S T I O S
A N O I B A G N Y I A L C T
L I H N L H R H O S U G T E
U C I L A U G H T T T D R I V
E K O E A D V I C E A E S E
S R Q B R O T H E R R E C N
Y P P I K S Y O U N G D K Z
```

Solution on Page 322

AMPLITUDE

ANALOG

ANTENNA

AUDIO

BANDWIDTH

BEAM

BROADCAST

CABLE

CAPACITOR

CHANNEL

CIRCUIT

COLOR

COMPONENT

CONVERTER

COPPER

CRT

CURRENT

DETECTOR

DIGITAL

DIODES

ELECTRON

FREQUENCY

HDTV

IMAGE

INDUCTOR

MODE

OSCILLATE

PHASE

PROCESSED

RECEIVER

SIGNAL

SPEAKER

SPECTRUM

TUBE

TUNER

VIDEO

WAVES

WIRELESS

```
P W L C U R R E N T H O L N
H R A E C R O T I C A P A C
A D O V N A E G A M I C N O
S I R C E N B B P I K O G L
E G E R E S A L U J R M I O
S I C B E S I H E T V P S R
P T E A F T S A C D A O R B
E A I N U F R E Q U E N C Y
A L V D D D L E D C W E I A
K R E W O E D I V I R N R N
E E R I Q O T G R N D T C T
R P B D M T O E O U O H U E
E P E T A L L I C S O C I N
N O A H A E D T V T D H T N
U C M N S U O S E D O I D A
T U A S A R S P E C T R U M
```

Solution on Page 322

ADAPTER

AMPLIFIER

CABLE

CART

COMPUTER

CONSOLE

CORD

ELECTRICITY

HEADPHONE

INTERACTIVE

LAPTOP

LIGHTS

MICROPHONE

MIXER

MONITOR

MOUNT

OVERHEAD

POWER

PRESENTATION

PROJECTOR

RADIO

REMOTE

SCREEN

SPEAKER

STEREO

SYSTEM

TELEVISION

TRIPOD

VIDEO

VIEW

```
A S Y S T E M O U N T R W T
R D D E H E A D P H O N E R
U O A G P L I G H T S L N I
M S E P O W E R I N E D O P
I N H F T I F N M V I I I O
X I R R P E O V I N C O T D
E C E F A M R S T Q O R A R
R O V M L V I E W G M E T O
E N O H P O R C I M P I N C
K S B B N A Y S T U U F E G
A O E T C P F C R U T I S M
E L Y T I C I R T C E L E A
P E I R O T C E J O R P R S
S V V A R M O E D I V M P Q
E X T C X R E N E L B A C L
X Z F Q S T E R E O I D A R
```

Solution on Page 322

ACTION

ACTORS

ACTRESSES

ADVENTURE

ANIMATED

BIOGRAPHY

BLOOPERS

BONUS

BUY

CARTOONS

COMMENTARY

DISNEY

DOCUMENTARY

DRAMA

ENTERTAINMENT

FAMILY

FANTASY

FOREIGN

LEARNING

MEDIA

MUSICAL

MYSTERY

NETFLIX

OUTTAKES

PIRACY

REDBOX

RENT

REPLAY

SERIES

SHOW

SONY

SUSPENSE

TELEVISION

THRILLER

TOSHIBA

VIEW

```
S P I R A C Y A L P E R Y F
R S E E M D E T A M I N A A
O E S D A B G E L Y O H C N
T R N B R L N L A S Q T U T
C I E O D O I E C T R S O A
A E P X O O N V I E W N C S
D S S F C P R I S R O O R Y
V X U K U E A S U Y M O E L
E I S F M R E I M M E T L I
N L E D E S L O E H D R L M
T F K I N S U N O B I A I A
U T A S T M T W U X A C R F
R E T N A A B I H S O T H W
E N T E R T A I N M E N T O
N B U Y Y H P A R G O I B H
T F O R E I G N O I T C A S
```

Solution on Page 323

AMATEUR

BAPTISM

BASEBALL

BBQ

BIRTHDAY

CAMCORDER

CAMERA

CARTRIDGE

CASSETTE

CHILDREN

CHRISTMAS

DIGITAL

EDIT

EVENT

FAMILY

FOOTAGE

FRIENDS

GRADUATION

LIGHTING

MEMORIES

MICROPHONE

MILESTONES

PARTY

PETS

PRANKS

RECORD

REEL

REUNION

SHOOT

SILLY

SOCCER

SPECIAL

TAPE

TRIPOD

VACATION

VIEW

WATCHING

WEDDING

```
A G V A C A T I O N T L P Y
M S I T P A B S P E C I A L
B B Q V D A R E M A C G R L
S A C H R I S T M A S H T I
O S T E P T N C R M T T Y S
C E N O H P O R C I M I E D
C B S R X R I O D L D N T N
E A E U D A T E H E I G T E
R L I E O N A W Y S G N E I
E L R T P K U A L T I I S R
C V O A I S D T I O T D S F
O I M M R H A C M N A D A L
R E E A T P R H A E L E C E
D W M R E I G I F S S W S E
C H I L D R E N O I N U E R
P B F O O T A G E V E N T D
```

Solution on Page 323

ACTRESS

ALLERGY

APARTMENT

BERNADETTE

BRILLIANT

CALIFORNIA

COLLEAGUES

COMIC BOOKS

COMPUTER

COOPER

DOG

ECCENTRIC

ELEVATOR

ENGINEER

FRIENDSHIP

GEEK

GENIUS

GIRLFRIEND

HOFSTADTER

HOWARD

JIM PARSONS

NERDS

OMAHA

PASADENA

PENNY

PHYSICISTS

PROJECTS

RAJ

ROOMMATES

SCIENTIST

WAITRESS

WOMEN

200

```
A G C O M I C B O O K S L L
H H B P A S A D E N A N T T
A O C I R T N E C C E O N B
M F G H P R O J E C T S E J
O S S S E R T C A J A R M Q
A T C D C O O P E R N A T Q
W A I N R O F I L A C P R S
O D E E O M R R D B O M A U
M T N I T M E E W R L I P I
E E T R A A T E A I L J A N
N R I F V T U N I L E H L E
E Y S L E E P I T L A O L G
R N T R L S M G R I G W E E
D N Q I E C O N E A U A R E
S E G G O D C E S N E R G K
G P H Y S I C I S T S D Y E
```

Solution on Page 323

ATHLETE

BILLY

BLUE DECKERT

BOOK

BUDDY

COACH

CONNIE BRITTON

DEREK PHILLIPS

DILLON

ERIC

FILM

FOOTBALL

GAIUS CHARLES

GARRITY

JASON

JESSE PLEMONS

JULIE

KYLE CHANDLER

LANDRY

LYLA

MAC

MINDY

PANTHERS

SCOTT PORTER

STUDENT

TAMI

TAYLOR

TEAM

TEXAS

TIM

TYRA

VICTORY

WIN

ZACH GILFORD

```
T Y H P T I M A T E X A S B
J E C H S F I L M I T P W P
L L A N D R Y T N E D U T S
S N O M E L P E S S E J R C
Y U C S R E H T N A P O A O
D K Y L E C H A N D L E R T
N N A S K A L Y L Y M J Y T
I O D Q P S L I A C A U T P
M S A T H L E T E O C L L O
G A R R I T Y R O T C I V R
U J F B L U E D E C K E R T
D R O F L I G H C A Z H I E
C O N N I E B R I T T O N R
K U R R P N O L L I D L I B
G A I U S C H A R L E S W H
Q L L A B T O O F B U D D Y
```

Solution on Page 323

ARTIST

ASSISTANT

ASSOCIATE

BOOM

BUDGET

CAMERA

CASTING

CHYRON

COSTUME

DESIGNER

DIRECTOR

DOLLY

EDITOR

EXECUTIVE

FINANCIAL

FOLEY

GAFFER

GALLERY

GRAPHICS

GRIP

IDEAS

KEY

LEGAL

LOCATION

MANAGER

MATTE

MIXER

OPERATOR

POST

PRODUCER

RUNNER

SET

SOUND

STORY

STUNTS

SWITCHER

TEAM

TITLES

VISION

WRITER

```
S W P I R G H M F X C Q R S
T R R G M M U O A O M O O B
N I O N Q A L A S N L V T C
U T D I R E C T O R A S I A
T E U T Y T U P E S I G D M
S R C S Y M E N S T C K E E
W E E A E R G O R O N R A R
I N R C A I C A N R A L S A
T N A T S I S S A Y N O Y B
C U O E A G R A P H I C S L
H R D T C B M R E F F A G H
E X E C U T I V E M A T T E R
R S Q D F Y X N O I S I V P
L A G E L C E C H Y R O N O
S E L T I T R K S O U N D S
T S G A L L E R Y L L O D T
```

Solution on Page 324

ATLANTIS

BANSHEE

BELIEVE

BETAS

BITTEN

CAMP

CHOSEN

CRACKED

CRISIS

CULT

DADS

DEADMAN

DEREK

DOUBT

FLEMING

FRANKIE

HARRY

HELIX

LEGIT

MARON

MAYDAY

MOM

PLEBS

QUIRKE

RAKE

RECTIFY

REIGN

REWIND

RITA

ROGUE

SAVE ME

SEED

SINBAD

SIRENS

SPY

TURN

TWISTED

UTOPIA

VICIOUS

VIKINGS

```
Y G H H R D E T S I W T F E
B A N S H E E V E I L E B P
T T D I P E D K Z T I G E L
J L U Y M S G L C N Z T T E
U A Z O A E N N D A F L A B
Q N M S C M L A E M R U S S
K T N O G L B F R D A C I Y
T I Q G B N X O E A N D Y V
W S U O I C I V K E K F E V
P I I S T E S K X D I M U E
Y S R Y T R R N I T E T U X
T I K N E S O H C V O G I F
B R E W N R P E A P O L Z W
U C I K A R R S I R E N S D
O N F M A W U A O H R I T A
D A D S P R T T R S P Y J G
```

Solution on Page 324

ACTION

AMUSING

ANIMANIACS

ANIMATED

BATMAN

BEETLEJUICE

BUGS BUNNY

CABLE

CHILDREN

CLASSICS

CLEVER

COLOR

COMEDIC

COMMERCIAL

COUCH

EARLY

ENTERTAIN

FAT ALBERT

FAVORITE

GARFIELD

GARGOYLES

HEY ARNOLD

HILARIOUS

LAUGHTER

LESSONS

LOUD

MEL BLANC

MORAL

NEW

POPEYE

REMOTE

SPONGEBOB

STATION

TELEVISION

TOYS

```
R T S C E F A T A L B E R T
L E S S O N S T A T I O N E
G P M Q C U E I T H L B L L
N A O O G A C T I O N U O E
I D R P T R I H C E Y G U V
S E A G E E U N N C P S D I
U Y L M O Y J T A I A B L S
M B M H M Y E B C M N U O I
A O D I E R L N L E I N N O
C B L L T E T E A L M N R N
L E E A I T E R S B A Y A A
E G I R R H E D S L T L Y M
V N F I O G B L I A E R E T
E O R O V U C I C N D A H A
R P A U A A L H S C W E N B
A S G S F L E C O M E D I C
```

Solution on Page 324

BEING ERICA

BIG LOVE

DALLAS

DOC

DYNASTY

FALCON CREST

FAMILY

GILMORE GIRLS

JUDGING AMY

LASSIE

LIFE GOES ON

ONCE AND AGAIN

PARENTHOOD

PARTY OF FIVE

PICKET FENCES

PROMISED LAND

RAISING HOPE

ROSEANNE

SIX FEET UNDER

THE BIG C

THE MUNSTERS

THE SIMPSONS

THE WALTONS

UGLY BETTY

```
D R F A L C O N C R E S T Q
T H E S I M P S O N S L B O
L J U D G I N G A M Y R E I
E I U E N N A E S O R I I B
D S F P I U E L Y S U G N P
U N R E A J T I C O D E G I
G O A S G R T E S B B R E C
L T I L A O T H E S H O R K
Y L S Y D L E Y E F A M I E
B A I T N E L S O B X L C T
E W N S A W S A O F I I A F
T E G A E Q X I D N F G S E
T H H N C Y L I M A F I C N
Y T O Y N B I G L O V E V C
Y Q P D O O H T N E R A P E
T H E M U N S T E R S P L S
```

Solution on Page 324

ALMA

ANNA GUNN

BLOOD

BROTHEL

CALAMITY JANE

CHARLIE

CON

DAN

DOC

FRONTIER

GAMBLING

GOLD MINE

GREED

GUNFIGHTER

JEFFREY JONES

JIM BEAVER

JOANIE

JOHNNY

JUSTICE

KEONE YOUNG

KIM DICKENS

LEON

MANIPULATION

MARTHA

MINING

MOLLY PARKER

OUTLAW

PROSTITUTE

SALOON

SETH

SHERIFF

SILAS

SOL

TOM

VIGILANTE

VIOLENCE

WHITNEY

```
N P J R E T H G I F N U G S
O N R E V A E B M I J N N H
O A U O F L G I L M U O I E
L D M G S F C O N O M E L R
A E A R A T R S Y A O L B I
S I N E L N I E R T O D M F
F L I E M L N T Y S O J A F
R R P D A O H A U J O M G E
O A U S E A L E H T O R B C
N H L K I M D I C K E N S I
T C A L A M I T Y J A N E T
I E T N A L I G I V H T E S
E N I M D L O G N I N I M U
R M O L L Y P A R K E R C J
E C N E L O I V Y N N H O J
Y E N T I H W A L T U O D K
```

Solution on Page 325

AGENT

ANGUS

ARCHENEMY

ASSASSIN

BERETTA

BOMB

CAPTURE

CULT TV

CUNNING

DICTATORS

ENEMIES

ENIGMATIC

ESCAPE

EXPLOSION

FIGHT

FOES

GADGETS

HERO

JUSTICE

KNIFE

LONER

LOST SON

MERCENARY

MILITARY

MORALE

MURDER

PETE

PHOENIX

PISTOL

QUIET

SCIENCE

SKILL

SOBRIETY

SOLUTIONS

SPY

TERRORIST

VILLAIN

VIOLENCE

WARRIOR

214

```
B M O B Y T E I R B O S C L
E E E E R U T P A C S H P Y
X C S R A T N E G A E D E R
I N C E T E R R O R I S T A
N E A T I E V K O C M E E N
E I P T L X H V T H E O C E
O C E A I P I A E E N F N C
H S R S M L T Y I N E I E R
P O R S L O P L U E G G L E
M V O A R S S O Q M L H O M
U K I S E I V S A Y J T I A
R N R S N O I T U L O S V N
D I R I O N I S T E G D A G
E F A N L C T O L L I K S U
R E W G N I N N U C U E I S
P I S T O L J U S T I C E M
```

Solution on Page 325

AMAZING RACE

AMERICAN IDOL

BIG BROTHER

BIGGEST LOSER

BLIND DATE

CASH CAB

CHEATERS

CHOPPED

COPS

DIRTY JOBS

FEAR FACTOR

GHOST HUNTERS

IRON CHEF

JACKASS

JERSEY SHORE

PAWN STARS

PROJECT RUNWAY

STORAGE WARS

STRANDED

SURVIVOR

THE APPRENTICE

THE VOICE

TOP CHEF

TRADING SPACES

```
J U I D I R T Y J O B S X O
E A M E R I C A N I D O L Q
R K M P J P A W N S T A R S
S E C A P S G N I D A R T D
E R S R E T N U H T S O H G
Y E C I T N E R P P A E H T
S S A T A C C T O J M S C K
H O S D D H I C P A A U H H
O L H E D O O E T C Z R E F
R T C D N P V J O K I V A E
E S A N I P E O P A N I T H
P E B A L E H R C S G V E C
T G A R B D T P H S R O R N
J G S T O R A G E W A R S O
O I O S F E A R F A C T O R
C B B I G B R O T H E R N I
```

Solution on Page 325

AMERICAN

ARTHUR

BARNEY

BILL MOYERS

BROADCAST

CAILLOU

CHILDREN

CLIFFORD

CORPORATION

CULTURE

DOCUMENTARY

FAMILY

FREE

FRONTLINE

FUNDING

GOVERNMENT

GRANTS

HISTORY

JIM LEHRER

KIDS

LEARNING

LOCAL

MUSIC

NATIONAL

NATURE

NETWORK

NONPROFIT

NOVA

PBS

RADIO

STATION

TELETHON

TELEVISION

VIEWERS

WGBH

WNET

218

```
A O I D A R U H T R A H L E
V K P B S T A T I O N B O B
O R B R O A D C A S T G C A
N O I S I V E L E T T W A R
E W L E A R N I N G Y O L N
R T L Y F R E E N A T U R E
D E M T R E R H E L M I J Y
L N O I T A R O P R O C V E
I A Y F N A T I O N A L I F
H C E O F R O N T L I N E U
C I R R N O H T E L E T W N
I R S P W U Y L I M A F E D
S E D N N E R U T L U C R I
U M I O E U O L L I A C S N
M A K N T N E M N R E V O G
G R A N T S C L I F F O R D
```

Solution on Page 325

ALEX TREBEK

ALLEN LUDDEN

ANOTHER WORLD

ARTHUR

CASH CAB

CURIOUS GEORGE

DICK CLARK

DONAHUE

GUIDING LIGHT

MEHMET OZ

MERV GRIFFIN

MUPPET BABIES

PETER MARSHALL

PRICE IS RIGHT

REGIS PHILBIN

RICHARD DAWSON

RUGRATS

SANTA BARBARA

THE DOCTORS

THE TODAY SHOW

THE VIEW

WORDWORLD

```
C K S R O T C O D E H T S X
R U E T P R Z O T E M H E M
P I R B A C H S A C E G I T
N R C I E R L F Y D P I B H
A E I H O R G H L L E L A E
R N D C A U T U Q E T G B T
A I O D E R S X R L E N T O
B F D T U I D G E Z R I E D
R F I H H L S D E L M D P A
A I C E A E N R A O A I P Y
B R K V N W R E I W R U U S
A G C I O P B W L G S G M H
T V L E D C W O O L H O E O
N R A W A R T H U R A T N W
A E R E G I S P H I L B I N
S M K W O R D W O R L D E A
```

ACTOR

CABLE

CARTOONS

CELEBRITY

CHANNEL

COMEDY

COMMERCIAL

COOKING

CREDITS

DOCUMENTARY

DRAMA

DVD

EVENTS

FINALE

FOOD

FRIENDS

GUIDE

HEAR

HISTORY

KIDS

LISTEN

MOVIE

NEWS

PREMIERE

REALITY

RELAXATION

RELIGION

REMOTE

SATELLITE

SCIENCE

SCREEN

SEE

SHOW

SITCOM

SOAPS

SPORTS

STATION

TELETHON

TV STAR

WATCH

```
G S F V H C T A W O H S W V
U E C N E I C S W E N Y P K
I S P O R T S O A P S T N I
D O C U M E N T A R Y I O D
E T C I E M L O O T D L I S
J E O C V O E A I R M A T C
Y L O A H E A R X G Y E A R
D E K B V R B S C A I R T E
E T I L L E T A S I T L S E
M H N E L I W D R O A I E N
O O G E D M N R O M S L O R
C N C E L E N N A H C R J N
T L R F I R S R E T O M E R
I C O R R P D N E T S I L P
S O F I N A L E C M O V I E
D V D G Y K K A E V E N T S
```

Solution on Page 326

AMY POEHLER

ANN SOTHERN

BLAIR BROWN

CATHRYN DAMON

CHARLOTTE RAE

DEBRA MESSING

EDIE ADAMS

GRACIE ALLEN

HELEN HUNT

IMOGENE COCA

JENNA ELFMAN

LAURA LINNEY

LORETTA SWIT

LUCILLE BALL

MARCIA CROSS

MARTHA RAYE

RHEA PERLMAN

SHELLEY LONG

SHEREE NORTH

TERI HATCHER

TINA FEY

TYNE DALY

```
S H E R E E N O R T H C T U
H E A R E T T O L R A H C L
E L Y T I W S A T T E R O L
L E G E Y A R A H T R A M A
L N N W O R B R I A L B C B
E H I M H T Y N E D A L Y E
Y U S Y E N N I L A R U A L
L N S E D I E A D A M S X L
O T E A C O C E N E G O M I
N A M F L E A N N E J M T C
G O A M Y P O E H L E R I U
N E R H E A P E R L M A N L
L X B S S O R C A I C R A M
R N E L L A E I C A R G F J
T F D R E H C T A H I R E T
N N R E H T O S N N A P Y Q
```

Solution on Page 326

AMAZING RACE

ANSWERING

BONUS

CASH CAB

CELEBRITIES

COMPETE

CONTESTANTS

DAYTIME

DOUBLE DARE

FAMILY FEUD

GAME

GSN

MONEY

NAME THAT TUNE

PANEL

PASSWORD

PLAY

PRICE IS RIGHT

PRIZES

PUZZLES

PYRAMID

QUESTIONS

QUIZ

SCANDALS

SCORE

SOLVING

SPONSOR

SURVIVOR

TEAM

THE MOLE

TRIPS

TWENTY ONE

```
S E L P Y E C E T E P M O C
N R C R S M O N E Y U F S R
O A V I P A N O P F Z A O O
I D M C I G T Y Y U Z M L S
T E H E R R E T R R L A V N
S L I I T T S N A O E Z I O
E B G S D H T E M V S I N P
U U N R U E A W I I U N G S
Q O I I E M N T D V N G Z E
H D R G F O T S T R O R I Z
S A E H Y L S N G U B A U I
C Y W T L E N A P S N C Q R
O T S E I T I R B E L E C P
R I N H M D R O W S S A P L
E M A C A S H C A B V Z P A
T E A M F S C A N D A L S Y
```

ACTOR

CABLE

CARTOONS

CAST

CHANNEL

DAY

DRAMA

EPISODES

FINALE

GUIDE

HOUR

LOCAL

MORNING

MOVIE

NAME

NETWORK

NEWS

PLAN

PREMIERE

PRIME

PROGRAMS

PUBLIC

RATING

REALITY

RECORD

REMINDER

RERUN

SCHEDULE

SERIES

SHOW

SITCOMS

SPECIAL

SPORTS

START

SUMMARY

SYNOPSIS

TIME

TITLE

UPCOMING

WEEKLY

```
U L X G E T Y T C I L B U P
G M O L N T T H I N S E P E
N C T C I I A R A M M A L L
I I A L A N N M A I C R A B
T N A R N L E R T T E E N A
A E X E T D G H O R S M Y C
R T L T I O L R E M Y I L H
E W I U R S O I O A N N K T
C O G P D W M N D X O D E S
O R L H S E D O S I P E E A
R K O A R N H W O H S R W C
D U L P I U P C O M I N G K
R N S M O C T I S E S U C T
A F I N A L E M S P O R T S
M O V I E A S P R I M E H Y
A M Y R A M M U S E I R M U
```

Solution on Page 327

ANGEL

ARCHER

BOSS

CHUCK

DALLAS

DEADWOOD

DEXTER

EPISODES

EUREKA

FIREFLY

FRIENDS

FRINGE

FUTURAMA

HEROES

HOMELAND

JERICHO

LOST

LOUIE

LUTHER

MAD MEN

MISFITS

MISSING

MONK

NEW GIRL

PROFILER

PSYCH

REVENGE

ROME

ROSWELL

RUBICON

SCRUBS

SEINFELD

SHERLOCK

SPACED

SUITS

TERRIERS

THE WIRE

VEGAS

WEEDS

WINGS

POPULAR SHOWS

```
K C U H C Q R O S W E L L X
L N D O O W D A E D Y J U W
K N O M V N E M D A M Z T E
B A H E D P L A O R S K H E
H S C L N E Q R S P A C E D
E A I A D E X U I E M O R S
R L R N Z L I T P G H L H S
O L E D Y M E U E L W R W O
E A J R E L I F O R P E I B
S D N E I R F S N L H H H S
T S O V D W T E S I R S G A
I C C E W T E R R I E R S G
F R I N G E D H S I N S M E
S U B G A S U I T S F G H V
I B U E U R E K A N G E L U
M S R E H C R A P S Y C H V
```

Solution on Page 327

ART

AUDIENCE

BEGINNING

BOOK

CHILDREN

CLIMAX

CONFLICT

CONVEYING

CREATING

CULTURE

DRAMA

EDUCATION

EMOTIONAL

ENDING

EPIC

FABLE

FAIRY

FANTASY

FICTION

FOLKLORE

GESTURE

GROUP

HERO

IMAGES

LEGEND

LISTEN

MUSIC

MYTH

NOVEL

ORAL

PICTURES

PLOT

SOUNDS

SPEAKING

STORY

TALE

TELLING

THEME

VOICE

WORDS

```
G E E S S P E A K I N G H N
O N C F G E S T U R E T W E
Q D I E A D R T M C Y Z B T
Y I O T N N A U I M A G E S
E N V U A L T S T H I D G I
R G O T E E U A E C U N I L
U S F J N M R R S C I A N E
T C I L F N O C A Y U P N V
L Y C W P L O T E D U B I O
U R T S K G I V I O O G N N
C I I L G O N E R O N A G L
I A O L N O N G K I N M B A
P F N T C C D C L I M A X R
E M R N E R D L I H C R L O
F A B L E G E N D T W D U E
W O R D S T O R Y Y E M E H T
```

Solution on Page 327

BABE

BATMAN

BIG

CAMILLE

CASABLANCA

CHINATOWN

CINDERELLA

DRACULA

DUMBO

FANTASIA

FARGO

FRANKENSTEIN

GODFATHER

GODZILLA

GRADUATE

GYPSY

HOLIDAY

HOUSEBOAT

JAWS

JEZEBEL

LASSIE

MASK

METROPOLIS

NOTORIOUS

PSYCHO

ROCKY

SABRINA

SCARFACE

SHANE

TOOTSIE

VERTIGO

```
G A L U C A R D S U S I Y Y
E R I M L E B E Z E J C K A
C I A S C A R F A C E C B A
F G S D A L L I Z D O G I N
V R D T U T V Q Q R K Y O I
E E A F O A N R G J A W S R
R H L N W O T A N I H C U B
T T L A K B T E F M B H O A
I A E M M E T R O P O L I S
G F R T B S N I D L B A R E
O D E A A U K S I Y O S O L
B O D B B O S D T H N S T L
M G N O E H A P C E V I O I
U R I Y A Y M Y D U I E N M
D A C N C A S A B L A N C A
L F E Y S P Y G B K S H H C
```

Solution on Page 327

ADOLESCENTS

ALARIC

BONNIE

BROTHER

CAROLINE

CENTURIES

CLAIRE HOLT

ELENA

EVIL

FANTASY

HIGH SCHOOL

HORROR

JENNA

JEREMY

KAT GRAHAM

KLAUS

MATT

NINA DOBREV

PAUL WESLEY

ROMANCE

SARA CANNING

SCHOOLGIRL

STEFAN

SUPERNATURAL

SUSPENSE

TEEN ANGST

TEENAGER

THRILLER

TYLER

VAMPIRE

VIRGINIA

WEREWOLF

ZACH ROERIG

```
A I N I G R I V N A F E T S
N Z A C H R O E R I G T U C
E K H Y L Y E R G W A P F T
L L I E A M V B N M E R A E
E A G L L E I O I R B E N E
W U H S A R L D N O J H T N
E S S E R E G A N E E T A A
R U C W I J T N A T N O S N
E S H L C U I I C Y N R Y G
W P O U R E W N A L A B Z S
O E O A C L A I R E H O L T
L N L P F M A H A R G T A K
F S G S T N E C S E L O D A
S E I R U T N E C N A M O R
C A R O L I N E R I P M A V
R E L L I R H T H O R R O R
```

Solution on Page 328

APATHETIC

CHAIR

CHIPS

COMFY

CUSHION

DOZE

FOOD

GAMES

IDLE

IMMOBILE

INFOMERCIALS

LETHARGIC

LISTLESS

LOAFER

LOUNGE

MOVIE

NAP

NEWS

PILLOW

RECLINED

REMOTE

REST

SEDENTARY

SIT

SLOTHFUL

SLOUCHED

SODAS

SPORTS

UNPRODUCTIVE

VIEWER

WATCH

Solution on Page

```
Y R I A H C H I P S A D O S
W N A P P H Y L J L Y U P A
M S L A I C R E M O F N I D
X E O T L T A T U T M P L E
Q T U H J A T H G H O R L R
F O N E F W N A A F C O O E
D M G T T S E R M U I D W C
F E E I Y I D G E L D U F L
L R H C E E E I S W L C U I
G S O C D I S C Q Y E T C N
J T J Q U V I M M O B I L E
F R E F A O L D N P N V V D
I O Z M T M L I S T L E S S
S P O Y J C U S H I O N W Q
U S D D H P G M R H T M A S
I H Q U Y I C C Z S O H K F
```

ABSURDISM

ALCOHOLIC

ALIA SHAWKAT

ATTORNEY

BALD

BLUTH

BUSINESS

BUSTER

CALIFORNIA

COMA

COURT

DAVID CROSS

GOB

HUSBAND

INCEST

JAIL

LINDSAY

LUCILLE

MAGICIAN

MICHAEL

MODEL HOME

NARCISSISM

PARENTING

PRISON

REAL ESTATE

RELATIONSHIP

SCANDAL

SIBLING

SOCIALITES

SPOILED

STUPIDITY

TOBIAS

TONY HALE

UNCLE

WILL ARNETT

```
N A I C I G A M O C G O B L
A A D J C T B U S I N E S S
R E L A T I O N S H I P G T
C S Y I V O L B P E L C N U
I C O L A I N O I C B A I P
S O A C Y S D Y H A I R T I
S U B L I E H C H O S E N D
I R L E I A N A R A C A E I
S T U A B F L R W O L L R T
M S T H D U O I O K S E A Y
B P H C C N V R T T A S P A
U O W I L L A R N E T T R S
S I L M T S E C N I S A I D
T L M S I D R U S B A T S N
E E L M O D E L H O M E O I
R D L A B D N A B S U H N L
```

Solution on Page 328

ACTION

ACTORS

ALONE

CABLE

CARTOON

CHANNEL

CHIPS

COMEDY

COUCH

DRAMA

DRINKS

FAMILY

FAVORITE

FRIENDS

FUN

GATHER

GUIDE

HUSBAND

LAUGHTER

LISTINGS

NETWORK

NEWS

PETS

PIZZA

POPCORN

REALITY

RECORD

REMOTE

RERUN

SERIES

SHOW

SNACKS

SODA

SPECIAL

SPORTS

STATION

TIME

VIEW

WATCH

WIFE

```
H C T A W F U N N W V W A E
M C X S K C A N S T E P R F
A A U D D R A M A Z Z I P I
F L C O N F D R I N K S T W
S R O T C A C R O L L K I H
U E G N I V B O U A Y K M J
S T H C E O T S U N U R E R
P O P C O R N G U E K K D V
O M B U A I H N Y H R S I Y
R E C C W T S I T F O P U D
T R A H E E W T I R W E G E
S Q B R I E O S L I T C A M
O R L R V P H I A E E I T O
D N E W S L S L E N N A H C
A S N D R O C E R D K L E X
S U U N O I T A T S M O R K
```

Solution on Page 328

AWARDS

BRUTALITY

CALIFORNIA

CAPTAIN

CLAUDETTE

CORRINE

CORRUPTION

COUNCILMAN

CRIME

CURTIS

DANNI

DETECTIVE

DRAMA

DRUGS

DUTCH

GLENN CLOSE

HARASSMENT

HOLLAND

JAY KARNES

JULIEN

JUSTICE

LAPD

LOS ANGELES

MURDER

OFFICER

PRECINCT

RONNIE

SHANE

STEVE

STREETS

STRIKE TEAM

THE BARN

THE FARM

THRILLER

VIC

```
D Z C D E T E C T I V E A G
N B O U P T L M J V T W E T
A E R F R A T U I C A E N H
L V N U F T L E N R V N I R
L E O J T I I I D G C A R I
O T I W E A C S L U I H R L
H S T N S E L E G N A S O L
A T P K R T N I R U E L C E
R E U P F N R O T C R I C R
A E R M C D F I I Y V D I D
S R R L U I M T K D R A M A
S T O T L U S T H E B A R N
M S C A R U T C A P T A I N
E H C D J A Y K A R N E S I
N H E Y C O U N C I L M A N
T R O N N I E T H E F A R M
```

Solution on Page 329

ADOLESCENT	JOE FLAHERTY
ALAN	KEN
BILL	KIM
BOY	MARTIN STARR
BROTHER	MILLIE
BUSY PHILIPPS	NEAL
CINDY	NERD
CLASSMATE BAND	NICK
DANIEL	SAM
DAUGHTER	SETH ROGEN
DAVE ALLEN	SISTER
FATHER	SON
FRANK	STEVE BANNOS
FRIENDSHIP	STUDENT
GIRL	TEACHER
GLASSES	TEEN
GORDON	TROUBLED
HAROLD	
HARRIS	
JEAN	
JEFF	
JERRY MESSING	

```
A J F T N E D U T S L Z D R
D O O R N O S A J E A N A E
T N M E A D O L E S C E N T
M R A A F N Z A R S M L I S
I L O B R L K N R A I L E I
L O N U E T A B Y L K A L S
L E I S B T I H M G J E F F
I R C Y S L A N E E T V N N
E R K P L D E M S R S A M E
R E T H G U A D S T T D B G
E H E I H A R R I S A Y O O
H T A L R I G E N K A R Y R
T O C I N D Y N G T D L R H
A R H P D N H A R O L D C T
F B E P I H S D N E I R F E
C I R S O N N A B E V E T S
```

Solution on Page 329

BONANZA

BROADCAST

CABLE

CARTOON

CHANNEL

CHEERS

CLASSIC

COMEDY

DAILY

DALLAS

DRAMA

DYNASTY

EPISODES

FAVORITES

FRIENDS

GAME SHOW

GUNSMOKE

HIT

LISTINGS

MARATHON

MEMORABLE

MYSTERY

NETWORKS

NIGHT

RECORD

REMEMBER

REPEAT

RETRO

SCHEDULE

SEINFELD

SERIES

SITCOM

TALENTED

WATCH

WESTERN

```
P Y T S A N Y D A L L A S D
C Y R E T S Y M H C T A W A
E S E I R E S I T C O M C I
N E C N O O T R A C U E I L
L T O F T N E T W O R K S Y
E G R E P I S O D E S O S H
N H D L B D W O H S E M A G
N I K D N R W N G S T S L C
A T G E G E O N T R I N C E
H Z I H S H I A E W R U C L
C R N T T T L M D C O G A U
F O E A S E E A O C V J B D
L R R I N M E M O R A B L E
N A L T B O E A N E F S E H
M H E E E D B R E P E A T C
E D R D Y R M D C H E E R S
```

Solution on Page 329

ADAM

BEN DANIELS

BLAIR

BRITISH

CARLY

CHRISTINA

CLAIRE

CONFLICT

CONGRESS

COREY STOLL

DOUG

DRAMA

DUPLICITY

FRANCIS

JANINE

JOURNALISM

KATE MARA

KEVIN SPACEY

LARRY PINE

LINDA

MANIPULATION

MICHAEL GILL

PETER RUSSO

POLITICS

PRESIDENT

RACHEL

RELATIONSHIP

REMY

ROBIN WRIGHT

STRATEGY

UNDERWOOD

WIFE

ZOE

```
Y Y G E T A R T S S S C T A
M T C I L F N O C L K N D D
E H D R A M A I E A E O Z A
R G U O D D T I T D O K X M
E I J A N I N E I S E M S Y
L R Q I L A M S S V I I L Y
A W L O D A E U I C L R E T
T N P N R R R N H A A B H I
I I E A P R S A N C L Z C C
O B T S E P E R I A L C A I
N O I T A L U P I N A M R L
S R E C G O B R I T I S H P
H P E I J D O O W R E D N U
I Y L L O T S Y E R O C E D
P L A R R Y P I N E F I W T
C O N G R E S S I C N A R F
```

Solution on Page 329

ABC

ALAN THICKE

BEN

CAROL

CLOSE

CRISSIE

DEBBIE

ED MALONE

EDDIE

FAMILY

JASON

JEREMY MILLER

JOANNA KERNS

JOURNALIST

KATE MALONE

KIDS

KIRK CAMERON

LAURA LYNN

LONG ISLAND

MIKE

MOVIE

NEW YORK

PROBLEMS

PSYCHOLOGIST

RAISE

RAMBUNCTIOUS

REPORTER

SEAVER

SHELLEY

SYNDICATION

TRACEY GOLD

TROUBLEMAKER

WIFE

```
M R T D L O G Y E C A R T N
T O A R N E W Y O R K S R O
I S V M O A C E L R I H E I
J M I I B U L L I G D E T T
O E I L E U B S O D S L R A
A L R K A N N L I S D L O C
N B E E E N O C E G E E P I
N O V B M H R L T M N Y E D
A R A Z C Y E U A I A O R N
K P E Y G F M D O M O K L Y
E E S I A R A I M J E U E S
R P L O R A C M L A E T S R
N O S A J U K B I L L F A H
S N N Y L A R U A L E O I K
A L A N T H I C K E Y R N W
D E B B I E K C R I S S I E
```

Solution on Page 330

ACTORS

ADVICE

AFTERNOON

AMUSING

BIOGRAPHIES

CELEBRITY

CENSORSHIP

CHILDREN

CLIFFHANGER

COMMERCIALS

COURT SHOW

DAILY

DRAMA

EDUCATIONAL

FAMILY

FLUFF

FOOD

GAMES

HEALTH

HOSTS

HOUSEWIVES

INFOMERCIAL

INTEREST

MARATHON

NETWORKS

NEWS

PRESCHOOL

REPEATS

SOAP OPERA

SUSAN LUCCI

SYNDICATED

TALK

```
Z P C A F T E R N O O N P O
A I W O R S N E T W O R K S
D H O D M E S R O T C A Y M
V S H R N M P D O O F N M C
I R S A E A E O F T D A H C
C O T M W G I R P I R S T H
E S R A S H N N C A E K L I
L N U E D U C A T I O N A L
E E O S P F T H H E A S E D
B C C K A E O P O F R L H R
R V L M D N A G S I F E S E
I A I A F R L T T J X I S N
T L I F G A M U S I N G L T
Y L U O P R E S C H O O L C
Y L I N F O M E R C I A L O
F B N N H O U S E W I V E S
```

Solution on Page 330

ACTION

ALEX

AMANDA

ASSASSIN

BERETTA

BIKINI

BOXING

COVERT

DIVISION

DOUBLE LIFE

ESCAPED

EXECUTION

FUGITIVE

GADGET

GIRL

GLOCK

HEROINE

KNIFE

KUNG FU

MAGGIE Q

MICHAEL

MURDER

NIKITA

NOAH BEAN

PERCY

PISTOL

REVOLVER

RIFLE

ROGUE

RYAN

SEAN

SECRET

SEYMOUR

SHANE WEST

SONYA

SPY

TAE KWON DO

TEENAGER

TOUGH

TRAINING

256

```
R G A P N B E R E T T A H M
E I S E A N D I V I S I O N
D R T R E V O C X S R T F O
R L E C B X E L A E E E U I
U U L Y H Y P S X Y V R G T
M T F D A B S E R M L C I C
K R I G O I C O E O O E T A
C A R X N U G Q G U V S I V
O I I I T U B N A R E E V Q
L N K I E E K L N W R F E T
G I O D N O W K E A T I S O
B N H E R O I N E L G N C U
N G T E G D A G T G I K A G
A Y N O S H S H A G R F P H
Y L O T S I P M I C H A E L
R E O N I K I T A M A N D A
```

Solution on Page 330

ANTHEM

ARCHERY

ATHENS

ATHLETE

ATLANTA

BEIJING

BOXING

BRONZE

CALGARY

COMPETE

CURLING

CYCLING

DIVING

FENCING

GAME

GOLD

HOCKEY

JUDO

LONDON

LUGE

NAGANO

OSLO

PODIUM

RACE

RINGS

ROME

ROWING

SCORE

SILVER

SKIING

SOCCER

SUMMER

SWIM

SYDNEY

TEAM

TOKYO

TORCH

VAULT

WINNER

WINTER

```
P Z E R O C S B F J M V M M
S W B I D Y R E H C R A E D
F I O N U K N I T M X U H M
H N X G J C B J U E U L T L
C T I S I W S I T T L T N Z
R E N N I W D N R E Z H A Y
O R G E I O W G O P A J T R
T U A H P E N N M M E M L A
T S M T C I A I E O G O A G
A Y E A W G W L B C U Y N L
G D R O A S S R S Y L K T A
O N R N U S O U I C O O A C
L E I M Q N Z C L L N T I L
D Y M I Z G N I V I D J Y X
C E Y E K C O H E N O L S O
R E C C O S N I R G N Q I J
```

Solution on Page 330

BARNEY MILLER

CHEERS

EXTRAS

FAMILY GUY

FAWLTY TOWERS

FRASIER

GET SMART

HAPPY DAYS

I LOVE LUCY

LOUIE

MODERN FAMILY

NIGHT COURT

RAISING HOPE

SCRUBS

SOUTH PARK

SPACED

SPORTS NIGHT

TAXI

THAT GIRL

THE COSBY SHOW

THE MIDDLE

THE MONKEES

THE MUNSTERS

THE ODD COUPLE

THE SIMPSONS

WEEDS

WINGS

```
S S R E T S N U M E H T T B
D R E L D D I M E H T R A S
E E P F R A S I E R U R K E
E W O S B U R C S O N T R E
W O H S Y B S O C E H T A K
I T G G T Y I T Y E T T P N
L Y N N A G H M O R H N H O
O T I I X G I D A A G Y T M
V L S W I L D M T S I U U E
E W I N L C S G E P N G O H
L A A E O T I X K A S Y S T
U F R U E R T E B C T L R E
C P P G L R T Y A E R I E I
Y L I M A F N R E D O M E U
E K H S S Y A D Y P P A H O
T H E S I M P S O N S F C L
```

Solution on Page 331

ACCOUNT

ACTION

BANDWIDTH

BIOGRAPHIES

COMEDY

COMPUTER

CONSOLES

CONVENIENT

DISCS

DOCUMENTARY

DOWNLOAD

DVD

FAMILY

FAST

FAVORITES

FEE

FITNESS

FOREIGN

GENRES

HISTORY

HORROR

INSTANT

MAIL

MEMBERSHIP

MOVIES

MYSTERY

POPULAR

QUEUE

ROMANCE

STREAMING

TABLET

TELEVISION

TRIAL

UNLIMITED

VIDEO

WESTERNS

```
L K Y L I M A F Q U E U E W
I F D T S A F H O R R O R E
A E E B M Y S T E R Y T C S
M E M B E R S H I P W E O T
B I O G R A P H I E S L N E
C F C F A T A O N E H E S R
T R I A L N C S G C I V O N
H E D V U E C E I N S I L S
T T V O P M O I E A T S E C
N U D R O U U V R M O I S S
A P A I P C N O O O R O S I
T M C T W O T M F R Y N E D
S O T E C D E T I M I L N U
N C I S R G N I M A E R T S
I D O W N L O A D O E D I V
G E N R E S T A B L E T F T
```

Solution on Page 331

ACTOR

ARTHUR

BEVERLY

BUSINESS

CAMEO

CELEBRITY

COMEDIAN

CREW

DARLENE

ENTERTAINMENT

FICTIONAL

GUEST

HANK

HBO

HOST

HUMOROUS

INTERVIEW

JEFFREY TAMBOR

JERRY

JOKE

LINDA DOUCETT

PARODY

PAULA

PENNY JOHNSON

PHIL

PRODUCERS

RIP TORN

SATIRE

SHOWBIZ

SITCOM

SPOOF

STAFF

WORKPLACE

WRITER

```
A H O S T K N A H P A P J F
M I E T Y Q A P U E L H E J
O H K A T E R F M N U I R E
C Y O F I C T I O N A L R F
T L J F R A H L R Y P N Y F
I R S E B L U I O J E A I R
S E W R E P R N U O O I L E
H V K O L K P D S H E D E Y
O E N T E R T A I N M E N T
W B S C C O X D R S A M E A
B T Q A P W J O T O C O L M
I S S E N I S U B N D C R B
Z E P R O D U C E R S Y A O
T U W E I V R E T N I H D R
M G H E N R O T P I R B B X
W R I T E R I T A S P O O F
```

Solution on Page 331

ADAM WEST

ALEC BALDWIN

ASHTON KUTCHER

BARBARA EDEN

BOB BARKER

CHRIS MELONI

DAVID SOUL

DIANE SAWYER

ELLEN POMPEO

EVA LONGORIA

HENRY WINKLER

HUGH LAURIE

JAY LENO

JIMMY FALLON

JIMMY KIMMEL

JON STEWART

KATIE COURIC

LEE MAJORS

LEONARD NIMOY

MARK HARMON

PAM DAWBER

RYAN SEACREST

TINA FEY

```
E L L E N P O M P E O G C J
S H R E Y W A S E N A I D A
O A I R O G N O L A V E C Y
P T N A H N T D U S Y R H L
B R O L U B A S O H E E R E
K A M E G O T R S T F B I N
A W R C H B S O D O A W S O
T E A B L B E J I N N A M L
I T H A A A W A V K I D E L
E S K L U R M M A U T M L A
C N R D R K A E D T R A O F
O O A W I E D E Y C K P N Y
U J M I E R A L D H J W I M
R Y A N S E A C R E S T P M
I R E L K N I W Y R N E H I
C Y Y L E M M I K Y M M I J
```

Solution on Page 331

ABSURDISM

ACCENT

ACTING

ANIMATION

BBC

BRITISH

CAST

COMEDY

ECCENTRIC

ENGLAND

ENGLISH

ENSEMBLE

ERIC IDLE

HUMOR

IRREVERENCE

JOHN CLEESE

LAUGHTER

MOVIES

MUSICAL

PARODY

PARROT

PERFORMERS

POLITICS

ROLES

SATIRE

SILLY WALKS

SINGING

SLAPSTICK

SONG

SPOOF

SURREALISM

TEAM

TERRY JONES

THE GOONS

THE PYTHONS

```
L F O O P S I N G I N G B C
A H Z O N O I T A M I N A B
C O M E D Y D O R A P S B B
I T O R R A P B R I T I S H
S S K L A W Y L L I S U U D
U N L A U G H T E R R S R N
M O O A C C E N T R I R D A
S H J O H N C L E E S E I L
L T E H G S K A R V C M S G
A Y L T S E L O R E I R M N
P P D E Y I H M Y R T O A E
S E I A S V L T J E I F C R
T H C M S O N G O N L R T I
I T I R O M U H N C O E I T
C I R T N E C C E E P P N A
K L E E L B M E S N E E G S
```

Solution on Page 332

ACTION	FUN
ADVENTURE	HORROR
AUDIENCE	INDIE
BLANKET	MUSICAL
CANDY	MYSTERY
CARTOON	PICTURE
CHOCOLATE	POPCORN
COMEDY	RELAX
COUCH	RENTAL
CREDITS	ROMANCE
CRIME	SCARY
DARK	SEATS
DATE	SHOW
DRAMA	SNACKS
DRINKS	SODA
EPIC	SOUND
FAMILY	THRILLER
FANTASY	WESTERN
FEATURE	
FILM	
FLICK	
FRIENDS	

```
U S Y W O H S O D A U C X M
N O H D I N R E T S E W A O
I U S K N I R D F A M I L Y
I N F E T A L O C O H C E D
L D E S R I C T C D B J R D
H R R D V U I X A P E G H C
N A U N O O T R A C O C I B
B M T E N H K N N R U P L S
L A C I S U M A E O E A K K
E M I R C Y M L C V N M C C
I H P F S O L R N K D W I A
D O S T R I E R E N T A L N
N R E F R D Q T I M L I F S
I R A H I G P Y D E M O C V
Y O T T F E A T U R E T A D
B R S C A R Y S A T N A F X
```

BARTENDER

BRAVE

CATTLE

CHESTER

COWBOY

CULT TV

DENNIS WEAVER

DEPUTY

DILLON

DOC

DRAMA

FESTUS

FRAUD

FRONTIER

GUNFIGHTS

HERO

JAMES ARNESS

KANSAS

KEN CURTIS

KITTY

LAW

MARSHAL

MATT

MILBURN STONE

PROBLEMS

RADIO SHOW

RESPECT

RUSTLING

SALOON

SIDEKICK

TOUGH

TOWN

VIOLENCE

WESTERN

WHISKEY

WILD

```
H N O L L I D K A N S A S B
G W D C D B S M E L B O R P
U O R U S T L I N G R W Y C
C O T A L R C R G O J A J T O
T R M T R E A U T L V A T W
F R A T E P D N S S E M I B
X E C V D S I F N I V E K O
S I H H N E O I R T I S C Y
A T E F E R S G U R O A I F
L N S N T R H H B U L R K E
O O T W R C O T L C E N E S
O R E V A E W S I N N E D T
N F R T B T T A M E C S I U
E Y T U P E D S F K E S S S
P L A H S R A M E C O D A F
E R C Y E K S I H W I L D N
```

Solution on Page 332

AIR

ALF

ANIMATED

ANTENNAE

BEWITCHED

BONANZA

CARTOON

CHEERS

CHIPS

COMEDY

DECADES

DRAMA

EPIC

FIFTIES

FILMS

FLIPPER

FONZIE

GILLIGAN

LASSIE

LUCY

MOVIES

MUNSTERS

MYSTERY

NETWORK

NEWS

NIGHTLY

POPULAR

PROGRAM

RERUNS

RETRO

ROSEANNE

SEINFELD

SERIES

SITCOM

SOAPS

THEME

WEBSTER

WEEKLY

WESTERN

WINGS

```
S C Y L T H G I N S P A O S
E S G N I W K R O W T E N Y
I P R O G R A M O M B H C R
R W E E K L Y S T U C U W E
E A T R U F I D R N L E N T
S C R P O T R D A S S N F S
E S O N C A L G C T A R O Y
C P Z O M E I A E E E E C M
H I M A F L B R S R E T O O
E H Q N L F N O Q S P S M V
E C I I R E R U N S I B E I
R E G M P S S E D A C E D E
S M E A N N E T N A N W Y S
S E I T F I F I L M S Z O W
Q H R E P P I L F L A X A E
N T I D E H C T I W E B F N
```

Solution on Page 332

AGENT

CBS

CIA

COMPUTER

CONSPIRACY

CRIMES

DETECTIVE

FINCH

FIXER

FUTURE

GENIUS

GOVERNMENT

HACKER

HAROLD

INFORMATION

JIM CAVIEZEL

JOHN

JONATHAN NOLAN

JOSS CARTER

KEVIN CHAPMAN

LIONEL

MOB

NYPD

OFFICER

PREDICT

REESE

ROOT

SECRET

SOFTWARE

SURVEILLANCE

TERROR

UNDERCOVER

VIGILANTE

```
G L F F R O R R R E T P Q Q T
E K F I X E R E E S E D D O
N O I T A M R O F N I J E O
I A P E T N A L I G I V T R
U P L I O N E L K M B N E E
S R J O H N H A C K E R C V
K E V I N C H A P M A N T O
T D M E N N V K N D A R I C
E I C I R I A R G L G E V R
R C F R E A E H L O E C E E
C T C Z I V W I T R N I D D
E C E B O M E T G A T F P N
S L I G F V E C F H N F Y U
N Y C A R I P S N O C O N D
R E T U P M O C B S S C J F
J O S S C A R T E R U T U F
```

A GIFTED MAN

BECKER

BEN CASEY

BODY OF PROOF

CHICAGO HOPE

CHICAGO STORY

CHINA BEACH

CITY HOSPITAL

CITY OF ANGELS

DOC

HART OF DIXIE

HAWTHORNE

INCONCEIVABLE

MEDIC

MENTAL

MERCY

NIGHTINGALES

NURSE JACKIE

ROYAL PAINS

SAVED

SCRUBS

SIDE EFFECTS

THE LISTENER

THE NURSES

THIRD WATCH

TRAUMA

```
N I G H T I N G A L E S G T
U N A M D E T F I G A N H W
R C H I N A B E A C H I L T
S O E I X I D F O T R A H H
E N C S A V E D R D T P S E
J C I B E Y R A W I H L I L
A E D U A E U A P A E A D I
C I E R K M T S W G K Y E S
K V M C A C O T N A G O E T
I A E S H H H H A H N F R F E
E B O D Y O F P R O O F F N
M L I T R O M E N T A L E E
E E I N Y E S A C N E B C R
R C E T H E N U R S E S T H
C H I C A G O S T O R Y S L
Y C H I C A G O H O P E R H
```

Solution on Page 333

ABU

AGENT

AMERICA

ATTACK

CARRIE

CHRIS

CIA

DAMIAN LEWIS

DANA

DAVID

HERO

HRACH TITIZIAN

IRAQ

JACKSON PACE

JESSICA

LANGLEY

MANDY PATINKIN

MARINE

MIKE

MORGAN SAYLOR

NAVID NEGAHBAN

NICHOLAS

OFFICER

PETER

PLOTTING

POLITICS

PRISONER

PROBATION

RUPERT FRIEND

SAUL

SERGEANT

TERRORISM

VIRGIL

WAR

```
R H E R O F F I C E R C O E
L D N E I R F T R E P U R U
A M A Q L G E N I R A M N S
N O B J A C K S O N P A C E
G R H E C R U B A K I N R R
L G A S I G I D C Z O D E G
E A G S R N T A I I A Y T E
Y N E I E I T T T M P P E A
D S N C M T I A I I O A P N
I A D A A T B A V K L T R T
V Y I F H O N N E E I I I L
A L V C R L A G E N T N S I
D O A P E P L U A S I K O G
W R N W W S A L O H C I N R
H E I R R A C H R I S N E I
M S I R O R R E T X Y P R V
```

Solution on Page 333

ALMONDS

BROWNIES

CANDY

CASHEWS

CEREAL

CHEESE

CHIPS

COFFEE

COOKIE

CRACKERS

CUPCAKE

DIP

DRINK

FRIES

FRUIT

GRANOLA

ICE CREAM

JERKY

MUFFIN

NACHOS

NUTS

PIZZA

POPCORN

POPSICLE

PRETZELS

RAISINS

RICE CAKE

SALSA

SANDWICH

SNACK CAKES

SODA

TEA

TRAY

VEGETABLES

```
E W S O H C A N R D A M S X
W D E S O D A L I F T R A Y
A N R O C P O P I Z Z A S E
E N K I A L O N A R G T L S
O I A H N C U P C A K E A E
E F L S V K C A S H E W S E
N F M R E A C C J I I C N H
E U O A G K P R Y E C P F C
R M N I E F A R A C R L S I
N G D S T R I C E C A K E W
D U S I A U C L K T K Z Y D
J Z T N B I S E A C Z E G N
S I J S L T E A C E A E R A
C O F F E E I H D I R N L S
G S T T S B R O W N I E S S
Y I F Y Q D F Q Y D N A C R
```

Solution on Page 333

ADULT

AUDIENCE

BAND

BED

CARSON

CELEBRITIES

CHIPS

CLASSICS

COMEDY

COMMERCIALS

CONAN

COUCH

FALLON

FERGUSON

GOSSIP

GUESTS

HORROR

HOST

INTERVIEWS

KIMMEL

LENO

LETTERMAN

LIVE

MIDNIGHT

MONSTERS

MOVIE

MUSIC

NEWS

NIGHTLINE

OPINION

OVERNIGHT

RERUN

SERIES

SHOWS

SKITS

SLEEP

SNOOZE

STEWART

TALK

VARIETY

```
N T S O H C I S U M G B H G
E E H F A L L O N I E C O S
W N O S U G R E F D O S R E
S I W V D Z S B V N S T R R
E L S A I U W A A I H S O I
I T A R E N E N P G L E R E
T H M I N A I D I H G U C S
I G K E C M V N X T C G H N
R I L T E R R C L C L O I O
B N A Y I E E O E A A P P O
E O T R V T T M M R S I S Z
L N L O O T N E M S S N H E
E E U L M E I D I O I I C N
C L D R C L R Y K N C O U H
T R A W E T S R E T S N O M
P E E L S R S T I K S B C Z
```

Solution on Page 334

ABC	NATURE
BET	NBC
BRAVO	NETWORK
CBS	NEWS
CINEMAX	OXYGEN
CNN	PBS
COMEDY	REALITY
COURT	SCIENCE
DISNEY	SOCCER
DRAMA	SPIKE
ESPN	SPORTS
FAMILY	STAR
FOX	STYLE
GSN	TBS
HBO	TLC
HGTV	TNT
HISTORY	USA
HOCKEY	WEATHER
HSN	
MOVIES	
MTV	
NASA	

O	V	F	N	I	E	L	K	N	L	K	Y	I	T
F	V	F	I	O	K	G	C	I	W	V	Q	N	W
E	C	Y	Q	A	I	M	O	V	I	E	S	P	N
M	A	J	L	Q	P	M	M	R	L	L	T	B	S
T	T	U	D	I	S	N	E	Y	L	Y	R	E	S
X	P	L	S	B	M	H	D	R	I	T	O	B	B
S	O	K	C	A	T	A	Y	K	A	S	P	K	T
A	W	K	I	A	S	Y	F	M	M	T	S	X	B
X	Y	E	E	A	E	R	U	T	A	N	S	T	Q
H	A	W	N	K	R	N	R	V	R	T	B	R	Q
Z	B	M	C	N	E	S	E	T	D	U	P	Q	O
I	Q	O	E	T	A	G	C	G	C	M	O	O	S
L	H	C	W	N	L	X	C	H	Y	B	F	C	N
Y	R	O	T	S	I	H	O	B	T	X	N	S	H
B	R	A	V	O	T	C	S	F	A	N	O	V	H
K	X	O	S	B	Y	F	P	N	A	K	T	L	F

Solution on Page 334

ALADDIN

ANIMANIACS

ARCHER

BATMAN

BEETLEJUICE

BLEACH

CODE MONKEYS

COWBOY BEBOP

DARIA

DEATH NOTE

DOUG

DRAGON FLYZ

FRISKY DINGO

HOME MOVIES

INVADER ZIM

IRON MAN

JOHNNY BRAVO

MEGA MAN

NARUTO

REBOOT

ROAD ROVERS

SOUTH PARK

SUPERMAN

TEEN TITANS

THE JETSONS

THE MASK

THE OBLONGS

THE TICK

```
A D Y Q S N O S T E J E H T
N F Z R I E T O N H T A E D
I K Y S O N I O W N F R T N
M R L G B A V V O O P C N I
A A F N E M D A O B S H A D
N P N O E A O R D M E E R D
I H O L T G U B O E E R U A
A T G B L E G Y A V R M T L
C U A O E M E N D T E Z O A
S O R E J B T N A A M R I H
G S D H U H Y H T M R A S M
T H E T I C K O E I N I N U
B L E A C H R J B M T O A K
N A M R E P U S S W A A R A
F R I S K Y D I N G O S N I
J S Y E K N O M E D O C K S
```

Solution on Page 334

ACTION

ASPECT RATIO

BROADCASTING

CAMERA

CLIPS

COMEDY

COMPRESSED

CONVERSION

COPY

DIGITAL

DIRECTOR

DOCUMENTARY

DOWNLOAD

DRAMA

DVD

EDUCATIONAL

ENTERTAINMENT

EXERCISE

FILMING

INSTRUCTIONAL

LABEL

MUSIC

PLAY

RECORDING

RENT

REPRODUCTION

RESOLUTION

REWIND

SECURITY

SHORT

SOUNDTRACK

STREAMING

WATCH

```
C O M E D Y T I R U C E S S
T R O H S T R E A M I N G L
I N S T R U C T I O N A L A
M R E P R O D U C T I O N N
U D O M R N B K P L A Y O O
S O D D N O R C J D I I W I
I W I C D I O A I O T P E T
C N G O I T A R T C E P S A
G L I M R U D T A U Q R I C
N O T P E L C D R M H E C U
I A A R C O A N E E C W R D
M D L E T S S U M N T I E E
L R A S O E T O A T A N X R
I A B S R R I S C A W D E E
F M E E C O N V E R S I O N
H A L D V D G B S Y P O C T
```

Solution on Page 334

ACE	HITTER
ASSIST	INNING
AXEL	JUMP
BLOCKED	LEADER
CHECKING	MULLIGAN
CONTROL	PERCENT
CROWN	PITCH
DEFENSE	PLAYOFF
DEUCE	POINTS
DOUBLE	REGIONAL
DRAFT	ROOKIE
DUNK	SLIDE
EAGLE	STRIKE
FIELD	TABLE
FINALS	TEAM
FORE	TREY
FOUL	TRIPLE
FRANCHISE	TROPHY
FUMBLE	
GOAL	
GUARDS	
HALFTIME	

```
J G G T M O H T A B L E G B
U F O F U S C N F I N A L S
M O H A L F T I M E S E Y M
P R X R L M I H L S Q L H E
Z E E D I A P O I I R G P D
L T C D G E R S U H E A O I
U M U J A T T S N C G E R L
O D E S N E F E D N I K T S
F O D O F C L V I A O I D S
J U C I K T R K V R N R L C
T B E L Y N C O Q F A T R T
B L O C K E D E W U L S K R
D E A A H C R C G N I N N I
E H N C C R E T T I H J U P
R O O K I E L B M U F H D L
S T N I O P L A Y O F F J E
```

Solution on Page 335

ADAM SCOTT

AMY POEHLER

ANN

APRIL

AUBREY PLAZA

BEN

CHRIS

DONNA

EMPLOYEE

FOURTH WALL

JERRY

JOB

LESLIE

MOCKUMENTARY

OFFICE

PARK

POLITICS

RELATIONSHIP

RETTA

RON

SATIRE

SITCOM

TOM

WORKPLACE

Solution on Page 335

```
W F L P A T T E R Q X O D J
M B S I U A E M N W K S F M
U N J H B D S C I T I L O P
Z E F S R A A W I R Y C U C
A T X N E M T E H F K J R I
H N W O Y S I C F U F D T T
D H W I P C R W M R E O H O
I N G T L O E E Q E M N W E
Z N H A A T N I K C P N A V
J Z X L Z T A L D A L A L Q
J H W E A N N S T L O Q L J
I T S R E L H E O P Y M A M
N V Y K I Y C L B K E H T Q
M Z L R N G G Y R R E J O B
V P P O Y S I T C O M X M G
P A R K D N Y F W W R N R R
```

Solution on Page 335

ACCOMPANIMENT

ACOUSTIC

ALTERNATIVE

BAND

BASS

BEAT

BLUES

BRASS

CELEBRITY

CLASSICAL

CONDUCTOR

COUNTRY

FOLK

FREE

GIG

GUITAR

HALL

HIP HOP

INDIE

INSTRUMENT

JAZZ

KIDS

LATIN

LIGHTS

METAL

MUSIC

ORCHESTRA

PERCUSSION

PIANIST

POP

RECITAL

SAXOPHONIST

SHOW

SING

SOUL

STAGE

STRINGS

SYMPHONY

Solution on Page

```
B H L H S T H G I L G I G X
R A Z Z A J P U N F O L K M
A L R E Z O E I D N I A A W
S L B S H A R T S E H C R O
S S T P A D N A B P C I U H
S B I E E X G R C O Q S M S
A H Y N R R O M M P L S S C
B R L R G N C P U S A A G E
P O B A T Y A U H S T L N L
I T B N T N N T S O I C I E
A C F L I I U O I S N C R B
N U R M U M C O H V I I T R
I D E D R E E E C P E O S I
S N E O I N S T R U M E N T
T O X K I D S T A G E Y Z Y
A C O U S T I C I L U O S G
```

Solution on Page 335

Answers

CHANNEL SURFING

1970S TV SHOWS

EUREKA

AWARD-WINNING TELEVISION

ON THE NEWS

1960S TV SHOWS

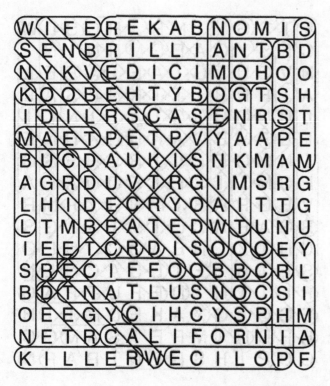

THE MENTALIST

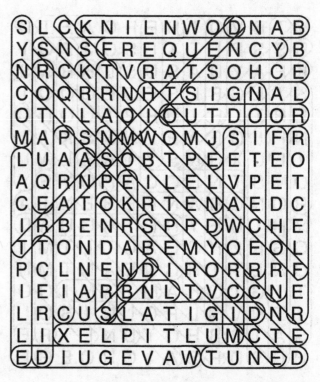

SATELLITE TELEVISION

TV WITH FRIENDS

PUSHING DAISIES

THE GOLDEN GIRLS

WHITE COLLAR

302

THE BACHELOR

TALK SHOWS

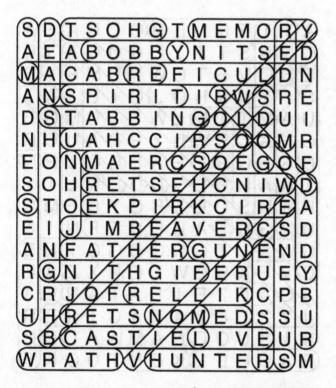

SUPERNATURAL

SPORTS NIGHT

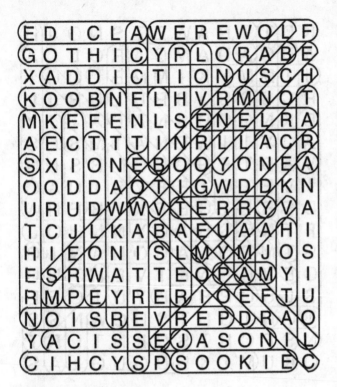

TRUE BLOOD

SONS OF ANARCHY

CABLE NETWORKS

JUSTIFIED

DEVOTED FANS

TV ADVERTISEMENTS

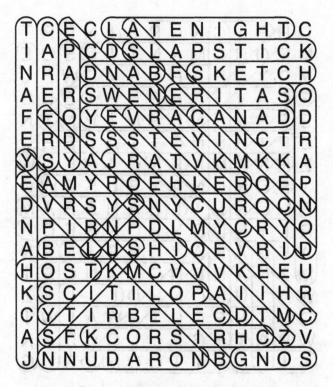

SATURDAY NIGHT LIVE

ACTORS IN DRAMAS

ANGER MANAGEMENT

STATIONS THAT START WITH A *W*

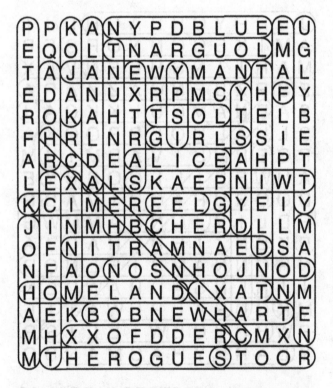

GOLDEN GLOBE AWARD WINNERS

HOW I MET YOUR MOTHER

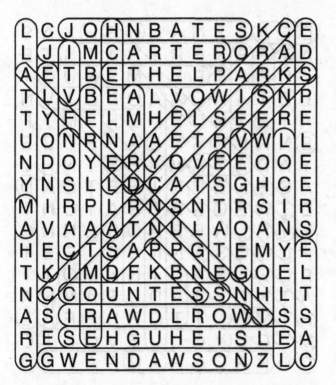

DOWNTON ABBEY

TV TIME

BURN NOTICE

WATCHING COLLEGE SPORTS

iCARLY

WATCHING GOLF

TELEVISION THROUGH
THE YEARS

BAND OF BROTHERS

308